HOW TO TALK TO A CAT

NEW JEWISH PHILOSOPHY AND THOUGHT
Zachary J. Braiterman

HOW TO TALK TO A CAT

Buber, Philosophy, and Dialogue with Unspeaking Things

Dustin N. Atlas

INDIANA UNIVERSITY PRESS

This book is a publication of

Indiana University Press
Herman B Wells Library
1320 East 10th Street
Bloomington, Indiana 47405 USA

iupress.org

© 2026 by Dustin N. Atlas

All rights reserved
No part of this book may be reproduced or utilized in any form or by any means, electronic or mechanical, including photocopying and recording, or by any information storage and retrieval system, without permission in writing from the publisher.

For customers in the European Union with safety or GPSR concerns, please contact Mare Nostrum Group B.V., Mauritskade 21D, 1091 GC Amsterdam, The Netherlands. Email: gpsr@mare-nostrum.co.uk.

First Printing 2026

Cataloging information is available from the Library of Congress.

ISBN 978-0-253-07576-5 (hardback)
ISBN 978-0-253-07577-2 (paperback)
ISBN 978-0-253-07579-6 (ebook)

*This book is dedicated to my father. I love him.
There is no way he would have ever read this.
But he would have talked about it.*

CONTENTS

Acknowledgments ix

Introduction: Dialogue and the Maintenance of Domestic Bubbles   1

1 Homes: Domesticity and Conflict   14
2 Animals: Communication and Language   25
3 Domestic Cats: Anxiety and Singularity   39
4 Plants: Dispersion and Surfaces   58
5 Babies: Noise and the Nursery   77
6 Sensuality: Tools, Crafts, Decoration   95

Conclusion: Death and Dialogue   111

Notes   115
Bibliography   145
Index   153

ACKNOWLEDGMENTS

This is a covid-19 book and a death book. It was conceived when I was confined to my house. It was written as my best friend, then my mentor, and then my father, all died. It was pulled together after the worst of this was over, when I learned that it is easier to write when sad than afraid. It is for these reasons a small book, at least in intention. It is also a first book, and so many of the ideas here have been simmering away for unseemly lengths of time. It would be impossible to thank everyone involved because that would include everyone I know.

Consider this an incomplete list of those who have read any part of this book or helped hold me upright as I brought it to completion: Bernie Zelechow, who taught me how to think; Meghan Henning, who worked over every inch of this godforsaken thing (except the baby chapter because she hates babies); Elliot Wolfson, for his dark and glowing mind; the angelic Ron Margolin; Zachary Braiterman, for his editing and cheerleading; Sharday Mosurinjohn for rescuing me from the evil empire; Emily Filler, Gregory Kaplan, Eli Horesh, Peg Olin, Sandra Yocum, Jeffrey Kripal, Alexandra Zirkle, Susannah Heschel, Adi Dajani, Derek Woods, Yaniv Feller, Jeremy Milloy, Jeffrey Bernstein, Adam Black, Sarah Imhoff, the adorable Poker Patrol, Myrna Gabbe, Jacob Mills, Larisa Reznik, Erik Davis, Josh Garoon, TKG, My mom, my siblings, Bob Erlewine; my brilliant, beautiful, and chaotic wife, Rebecca; my monstrous children, Gabriel and Ramona; and my beloved dead cat, Gimli.

HOW TO TALK TO A CAT

INTRODUCTION

Dialogue and the Maintenance of Domestic Bubbles

Martin Buber was a Viennese philosopher, a theater director, an aesthete, a cat lover, and a Jew. Like many of the fin de siècle set, he had a hunger for immediacy which clashed with an internalized Germanic culture of weight and precision, one sustained by a near-constant ingestion of books. Read from a present where it seems like nobody reads, the fear of the written word that permeated Buber's world seems quaint, if not delusional. But if we transfer that fear from books to screens it's more understandable and helps explain why Buber pits dialogue against the world of the grid: the world where everything has its place, whether on a page, in a network, or as part of a model.[1] In rejecting the grid, Buber has lots of company, good and bad, but he stands apart because his work on dialogue and is neither mystifying nor irrational. Buber's writing can be treacly or fantastical, but his ideas are not. Dialogue is strange, but not irrational; relationships are confusing, but not incoherent, and while we may have grown unaccustomed to reasoning about these matters, that does not make them unreasonable.

This book is about dialogue with entities that don't use language. In simple terms, it's about talking-to creatures that don't speak.[2] Talking-to them, not talking-about them.[3] But what is this "dialogue," and how much does it differ from the standard definition of the word? Buber's notion of dialogue (*Zwiesprache*) is modeled on human conversation but covers much more than discussion. Dialogue is bigger than conversation, but sparser in detail. If we strip dialogue down to the beams we can define it like this: *Dialogue is an attentive and reciprocal relationship, a relationship where we are directed toward another creature.* Conversation is just one type of dialogue, although it is perhaps the easiest way into the concept.

Let's break it down a little further. Dialogue is a *relationship* that is more important than its content. You can have dialogues without content as easily as you can have content without dialogue.[4] But because dialogue is reciprocal there is usually an attempt to pass something back and forth between the partners. Dialogue is *attentive*, which means we must be paying attention to our partner; dialogue is directed toward another creature. Dialogue is when I talk *to* you, not *about* you.[5]

In the most general and haphazard sense, talking-to is what distinguishes dialogue from analysis. Talking-to is the starting point for dialogue; talking-about is the starting point for critical thought.[6] This grammatical distinction (*to* vs. *about*, second person vs. third person) corresponds to two different stances toward a thing, stances you can probably intuit. Talking-about is relatively easy to understand. Talking-to is trickier: *How* do you talk to a cat? A machine? A plant? The dying? In each case, and for each type of creature, we do it differently. Not all mute beings dialogue in the same way. One goal of this book is to think about these differences and how they illuminate the structure of dialogue.

This definition of dialogue has a lot of moving parts. For this reason, it is difficult for us to *begin* with a precise notion of what dialogue *is*, as much of this book will be taken up with illustrating and exploring the definition's various parts. It is, however, relatively easy to say what dialogue is *not*. Specifically, it is not Buber's more famous I-You (or I-Thou) encounter, even if the two concepts share some characteristics. The I-You is an *encounter* where presence, or being there, is the most important thing. Dialogue is dynamic, a *process* that takes place over time and can move from place to place, and where *attention*, not presence, is central. This distinction between dialogue and I-You is rarely, if ever, made. Indeed, most of the works that claim to be about Buber and dialogue don't deal with dialogue at all but rather with the near ecstasy of the I-You encounter.

Both dialogue and encounter share the second-person stance, and for both the relationship is more important than the information exchanged within it. But the I-You encounter is more a function of grace, whereas the dialogue is a creature of will. Arguably, more work goes into dialogue, not only the effort of paying attention but also the cultivation of spaces, times, and states of mind where dialogue can take place. This book focuses on one set of these spaces—the domestic—as a key space for understanding dialogue and how we cultivate and maintain it. The I-You encounter can happen anywhere, although it seems to favor the bucolic and the natural. Plato, however, puts dialogue in the city: "The country places and the trees won't teach me anything, and the people in the city do."[7] Buber takes a middle path: Dialogue is urbane, but the trees may well have something to teach you.

In both the city and the country we dialogue with nonhumans, but no matter how inhuman our partners dialogue itself remains half-anthropocentric because one participant in any dialogue we can understand is going to be a human.[8] Antianthropocentrism is in fashion—and for good reason—but dialogue is not going to be part of that project. We may decenter ourselves when we engage nonhumans (we might even do it with another person), but our all-too-human concerns are always there. So, for instance, when we say that dialogue is attentive, this attentiveness only applies to us—a plant cannot attend to us in any way we are likely to understand. When we say dialogue is reciprocal, the nature of this reciprocity—what this reciprocity is—is probably quite different with a human baby than with a cat. This is why it is important to stress the *we* in the previous definition: How we comport ourselves in a dialogue might be very different from how our partner does.

But there is a basic problem. This is a book, an academic one at that, so there is no serious dialogue here. In general, books talk-about stuff; they don't talk-to you. So I will be writing-about the way we talk-to things, which is as stilted and confusing as it sounds. And it's a problem because this book is about talking-to creatures, but no amount of talking-about is going to get us to talking-to. Buber tries to get around this problem in several ways: evocative prose, biographical sketches, vignettes, and indexing (pointing at things).[9] His works try to pull you into a dialogical situation, or at least to play-act one, so you understand what he is talking about.

In this book, I limit myself to thought experiments, examples, and indexing (pointing). Pointing, whether with your index finger, a pronoun, or a description, is an essential element of Buber's philosophical presentation. As Peirce has elegantly noted, pointing allows us to distinguish between a fantasy world and the real one, between our ideas of dialogue and real dialogues: "The real world cannot be distinguished from a fictitious/imaginary world by any description. Hence the need of the pronouns and indices, and the more complicated the subject the greater the need of them."[10] When we talk-about a dialogue, we remain fully within the world of theory: Only by pointing at actual or potential relationships can we start to think about dialogue's real effects and conditions. A metaphysical castle is a beautiful thing, but if I cannot point to where it stands, we grow justly suspicious of its ability to shelter us. So we start off by pointing at a dialogue and then ask: How the hell does that happen and what does it look like when we trace its details?

The dialogues I point at occur in (or around) my house, with the domestic cat as the central case.[11] There are several reasons for this limitation, not least of which is that I wrote this book during a pandemic, so my observations were largely limited to domestic relationships. But there is an academic reason for this interest in our small worlds. Domestic worlds allow us to address a thorny issue in Buber: How do you encourage relationships? How do you make them *more likely to happen*? Buber knows that dialogue can and must be cultivated, but he rarely addresses the problem in detail: Why do some things and some spaces render us more open to dialogue than others do? How do we replicate these?

The work that goes into creating and maintaining the domestic space is familiar to us. The domestic bubble does not appear out of nowhere: It is built and maintained by manipulation, gossip, care, and near-constant labor. The home is not a state produced by fiat—it is a process and a place where beings of many sorts gather, grow familiar, and learn to love and despise one another. It is a place of many dialogues, including unpleasant ones. Finally, the slowness of the domestic is simply more in line with the tempo of dialogue than many other spaces are. As mentioned, dialogue has a different tempo and shape than the lightning flash of the epiphanic I-You encounter; it occurs more slowly, with pauses and interruptions, and it shares this with much of domestic life.

But how many types of domestic life are there, and how many variations of these exist in turn? I stick with three types of homes: an ancient model, the fin de siècle model (treated by Buber, Klein, and Freud), and my own. Again, this book was mainly compiled during the first years of the pandemic when many of us were bound to our homes and forced to appraise their details and mechanisms—whether we liked it or not. Also, while writing this book, I lived through several births and deaths, radical transformations of the home as singular as they are common. I suspect my home shares enough with yours—in a very general sense—that the examples I provide will be enlightening to you. If not, then the bourgeois home of the turn of the century is an "object" many of us are somewhat familiar with. Failing *that*, I hope the bare description of these experiences is enough to reference something familiar to you.

Why This Word?

The word in question is *dialogue*, or *Zwiesprache*. But why stick with this overused term, one worn near to death by human resources departments and wellness clichés? And why use a term that suggests speech, when the goal is to think about beings that don't speak?

I've a few reasons. First, *dialogue* evokes a common phenomenon, an experience we've all (hopefully) had: an intense, reciprocal, back-and-forth conversation. True, by dialogue, I mean something broader—a much larger set of relationships of which conversation is only a part. Dialogue is a type of relationship, and conversation is merely one type of dialogue. Still, for many, the experience of a powerful conversation is the easiest way to access the broader concept of dialogue. Like Buber, I merely extend the term so that it also covers relationships where there is no speech and where our partner is not human.

I suggest that normal conversations are only possible because they are part of a broader dialogue relationship. Further, much of what makes up what we informally call dialogue is *more* visible when we dialogue with unspeaking beings. I like the tension—bordering on paradox—of "dialogue with beings who do not speak"; the word *dialogue* illustrates both the trickiness of the relationship and the many obstacles to realizing it (or even just thinking about it). Using a different term just because *dialogue* now rings hollow feels defeatist—it seems better to restore the word's stolen dignity than surrender it to management.

Buber does have other words that could conceivably do the work *dialogue* does. He developed an extensive vocabulary to describe relationships of varying intensities, a vocabulary that transposes aesthetic and religious concerns into secular concepts.[12] So why use *Zwiesprache* (dialogue) instead of *Verhältnis* or *Beziehung* (both usually translated as "relationship")? Why not presence or the (unjustly) famous in-between?[13]

I believe dialogue is the best concept for reconstructing Buber's work in a manner that does not replicate the already existing quasihistorical studies, or those that inflate the I-You until it overpowers all of his other concepts.[14] I hope to save Buber from his fans—for whom he is a spiritual grandfather figure—as well as his detractors—for whom he is a muddle-headed dilettante. Buber is more of a rationalist than is generally conceded, and while he can be excessively evocative, he makes lucid arguments. The ecstatic elements of the I-You, especially when amplified beyond recognition by bad scholarship, obscure this.

Presence (*Gegenwärtig*) is another option, but it is a condition for dialogue and misses the active elements of the dialogue process.[15] *Realization* (*Verwirklichung*), the chief concept of the young Buber, is the opposite: It does not precede dialogue but follows it.[16] *Relationship* (*Beziehung*) is the most obvious contender, but it is far too broad; it includes everything from the most abstract association in thought to the most intimate connection. Dialogue is Goldilocks's favorite porridge: It is not as expansive as relation nor as intense and narrow as the I-You, but it is broad enough to include tools and housecats and narrow enough that we can exclude relationship that lack any encounter or mutuality.

The Philosophical Presuppositions of Dialogue: A Thought Experiment

I rely now on your intuitions to develop a fuzzy version of the concept of "encounter," which I will then clarify via a quick tour of Buber's little book *Dialogue* to help express what I mean by "dialogue." The intuition pump goes as follows: "Imagine a person that you have never met. Let's call her Emily. You know everything *about* her—absolutely everything: her past, how loudly she snores, her hair color, dreams, various infections, the moment of her birth, and the date of her eventual death. You know everything about her in the manner of a little god: Given any proposition about her, you know if it's true or false. So, a question: Even though you know everything *about* Emily, do you know her?"[17]

In other words, if someone asked, "Do you know Emily?" would it feel weird to respond with a "yes"? Most people I've spoken with think this would be weird; they would've said something like "No, you don't know *her*—you know *about* her."

Some people are comfortable saying, "Yes, I know Emily," but what does knowing mean here? Let's say that one day, you meet Emily in person and have a nice chat. Would you expect your exchange with Emily to alter your impression of her? You can't have learned anything *about* her—you already knew everything there was to know. But I'd guess that you now know her differently—but this difference cannot be propositional. It can't be a statement that can be true or false, or anything about Emily, because you already know all that stuff.

And that's the end of the story. It won't prove anything, and if anyone is dead set against thinking in these terms this won't convince them. For the rest: What is the difference in knowledge and relationship between thinking about Emily and encountering her? The difference cannot be thought of in terms of content or a proposition, at least insofar as nothing new is learned in an encounter. I think this is what Buber means when he writes,

> —What, then, does one experience of the You?
> —Nothing at all. For one does not experience it.
> —What, then, does one know of the You?
> —Only everything. For one no longer knows particulars.[18]

Here, "everything" is also a kind of "nothing"—or not-a-thing—because it is without particularity. This is why Buber (among others) cheerfully flips between "everything" and "nothing" when writing about encounter. We can leave the thought experiment with this: Something strange happens when you meet someone; this strange thing is also seen when you move from talking-about someone to talking-to them. This strange relationship is—with several caveats and modifications—an essential element of dialogue.

Of course, for Buber, the full I-You encounter is not a pleasant chat with an imaginary Emily; it is more intense and absolute. In the full encounter, all the stuff you know about Emily recedes and orbits around the singularity of your absolute encounter; she fills and dominates the world. This intensive exclusivity is the appeal but also the limitation of the I-You. Dialogue is a more expansive and composite thing.

Composition, Comprehending: The Place of Dialogue in Buber's Own Thought

For Buber, the I-You, the full encounter, is a real event. Like a movement, it is spatial and temporal, but not in the sense of a change in a time-space grid. Rather, the encounter *generates* space and time as its own abstractions, as if they were extruded from the event itself (this is typical of Buber, whose thought often emulates Leibniz's). The I-You is absolute and so is absolutely distinct from the I-It.

Dialogue is not so distinct. Dialogue, which is composite, involves fluctuations and varying states of intensity—from absolute encounter to total absence, dialogue is composite, it is impure, and "moments" can only be ingredients in a strange brew. Thus, we must say that dialogue takes place in both the It and the You.

As Buber aged, he became aware that the exclusionary logic of encounter created as many difficulties as it solved, but he remained committed to this exclusivity: Without it, his logic of relation falls apart. There must be some exclusive relationship to hold the fort, as it were; otherwise, everything collapses into the mass of thing-relations, and encounter is just a nice species of thing-relationship. How do *we* avoid an all-or-nothing approach when our focus on dialogue is less invested in exclusivity? By paying attention to degrees and intensities. As Buber writes in *Philosophical Interrogations*,

> Certainly, there is a graduated structure of I-It relationships where stage by stage the distance from the I-Thou relation becomes greater, and this structure is, by its nature, to a certain extent surveyable. But [even] Its highest stage IS unmistakably set in contrast to the realm of the I-Thou relation, since even there an objectification prevails for which is no room in this relation. A being to whom I really say Thou IS not for me in this moment my object, about whom I observe this and that or whom I put to this or that use, but my partner who stands over against me in his own right and existence and yet is related to me in his life.[19]

All the gradations occur on the side of the I-It: The I-You is absolute. Much of dialogue is thus I-It, in that it is close to the I-You—and crosses over into it—but is not identical to it.

Given that dialogue is not (only) exclusive, what then do we learn from the preceding digression, where we encountered an imaginary Emily? That digression articulates the logic of the encounter—or, rather, what is left out of the encounter by third-person accounts—but dialogue is not only encounter. Even the most transcendent dialogue probably involves moments of boredom or distraction. Dialogue is able to bind together encounter and boredom, presence and absence, because it takes place in the time of the everyday: "thoroughly dovetailed into the common human world and the concrete time-sequence."[20] It therefore requires a tolerance for fatigue and tedium. If anything, the best dialogue partners are able to endure or even welcome boredom as part of the process of talking-to someone or something. Dialogue is for those among us who are steadfastly unenlightened.

Dialogue's everydayness and lack of exclusivity make it confusing, if not muddy.[21] It is hard to discern what is dialogue and what is not. Yes, it's safest to assume most things aren't—and to bear in mind that not every discussion is dialogue.[22] But, conversely, not all dialogue is discussion, hence this book. "For a conversation [*Gespräch*] no sound is necessary, not even a gesture. Speech can renounce all the media of sense, and it is still speech."[23] We need not follow Buber to this extreme, and we rarely, if ever, will. I am a materialist by inclination and training (albeit one with an expansive notion of what it means to be material), so I stay close to the sensual world. But material reality involves subtle bodies and activities (such as perception and awareness) that are important for dialogue.

Dialogue is expansive and can be found in many strange places, including at work and at home: "A worker can experience even his relation to the machine as one of dialogue, when, for instance, a compositor tells that he has understood the machine's humming."[24] Disregarding the ludicrous and quaint way Buber describes labor, this concept is something many of us—perhaps most of us—can understand. You can have a dialogue with a car or a paring knife; in fact, you have probably already had a dialogue like that. I am concerned with how this is possible, how it happens, and what cultivates and sustains these dialogues. Why is it easier for me to have a dialogue with an old knife taken from a dead friend than one plucked from an Amazon bubble mailer? How do I talk to a cat? And how does the domestic cultivate these encounters?

Language of the Spheres

We cannot move beyond language by fiat. We are stuck with what it allows us to do, what it takes from us, and what it obscures. The distance from learning a language to a concept of death is a short one, almost as short as the one from understanding names to being able to see yourself as an object. These recognitions are part and parcel of the way language changes us, which allows people like Habermas to claim that self-consciousness originates in us talking to one another about something else.[25] Language viewed this way is not a skill but rather a cause *and* consequence of certain relationships. There is no language "in-itself" or outside of these relationships. As comedian George Carlin jokes, teachers might ask you to write something "in your own words," but that's impossible. You've spent your whole life using other people's words.[26] Language is shared or it's not language.

This shared thing (language), be it a process, tool, organism, or whatever, is one of the most obvious and concrete forms of relationship. That is why we use it and its forms as analogies and illustrations of other forms of relationship (is the computer talking-to the printer?). Here, it is "dialogue" we are using to understand relationships that are not constituted by language.

For Buber, "the limits of the possibility of dialogue are the limits of awareness," and yet few, if any, nonhumans use language proper. So we are left with the strange condition of dialogue with beings who don't have language.[27] But even as we use the word *dialogue* to describe these relationships, we can (and should) distinguish between dialogues that use language and those that don't.

This is why Buber offers three "types," or spheres, of relation that we can use to distinguish three kinds of dialogue.[28]

> Three are the spheres in which the world of relation is built [*baut*].
> The first: life with nature, where the relation sticks to the threshold of language.
> The second: life with men, where it enters language.
> The third: life with spiritual beings, where it lacks but creates language.[29]

It is unfortunate that Buber chose to call these *spheres*. I suspect he intended to show that these relationships come together, but they aren't spheres in any significant sense.[30]

The three spheres function in two ways: They help us categorize types of relationships and also act as a diagnostic, helping us determine the type of relationship we are in. If language is working, then we are in sphere 2; if we get stuck "before" language, we are in sphere 1; and if we find new words springing to mind, then sphere 3. In each sphere, the relationship is judged by how it fits, or doesn't fit, with human language. Nature sits at the threshold, humans exist in language, and spiritual beings (such as art and religious forms) make new language. I am almost exclusively concerned with sphere 1—the threshold. And even with this limitation, it is clear that sphere 1 is massive and undifferentiated. This is a problem if we want to explore nonhuman relationships. Buber seemed to notice this problem in 1957, when he added another layer to sphere 1: a threshold before the threshold, to distinguish between living and nonliving beings.[31]

We have three sets of relationships, with human language in the center, and two others (natural and cultural) identified as being "outside" of normal language. Again, Buber's simple formulation in *I and Thou* is in dire need of more distinctions. These distinctions are in large part a function of how language-like our relationships are. This is not to say that a housecat is more important than a volcano but that my relationship with a feline is going to be much closer in form to language than my relationship with molten rock.

But no matter how close to language a relationship gets, the breakdown of language that alerts us that we are in sphere 1 cannot be overcome.

The language-like nature of our animal relationships should not trick us into viewing them as being composed of some kind of language, however deficient. The relationships must be understood on their own terms: You are a language user, so language pervades but does not necessarily dominate the relationship. Buber illustrates this in his Hasidic tale, *The Language of Birds*. The Baal Shem Tov (the founder of Hasidism) gives Rabbi Arye the ability to "understand the language of all creatures" on the condition that Arye focus entirely on the creatures he is communicating with. Arye, predictably, tries to listen to the birds and the Baal Shem Tov at the same time, so he loses the power to understand the birds.

The Shape and Time of Dialogue (Slow Bubbles)

Dialogue, as I understand it, is broader and slower than the I-You encounter; it is less epiphanic and more procedural. For all its ambiguities, it is easier to analyze than the I-You, if only because it's easier to break into parts and organize into groups—the completeness of the I-You makes it something mysterious, indecomposable. "He is no longer He or She, limited by other Hes and Shes, a dot in the world grid of space and time, nor a condition that can be experienced and described, a loose bundle of named qualities. Neighborless and seamless, he is You and fills the firmament. Not as if there were nothing but he; but everything else lives in his light."[32]

Dialogue is less exclusive. It has seams and neighbors; it does not fill the firmament and can happen in corners.

Of course, our understanding of dialogue depends on our understanding of the I-You encounter: Dialogue passes into the I-You but then moves out again, hovering at the limits of the It and You worlds. Dialogue is composite—sometimes it enraptures our attention, other times it is meandering, boring, even dissociated. Indeed, the ability to work through boredom is as intrinsic to dialogue as it is to watching a long opera. Dialogue has to be cultivated and maintained because it takes up space and time in the It world as well as in the You-encounter; it has a tempo and needs a place to happen.

Buber describes a few intense encounters with trees, but a longer dialogue—say, over a season, where you can really see the tree respond to things—fades in and out. It takes a long time for a plant to show its reactions, and matching this pace requires leaving the intensity of the complete encounter. This process is also easier to explain than the epiphanic encounter with a tree. In his work on education—a long and laborious process if there ever was one—Buber most clearly articulates this: "A relation between persons that is characterized in *more or less degree* by the element of inclusion may be termed a dialogical relation. A dialogical relation will also show itself in genuine conversation, but it is not composed of this. Not only is the shared silence of two such persons a dialogue, but also *their dialogical life continues, even when they are separated in space*, as the continual potential presence of the one to the other, as an unexpressed intercourse."[33]

Just as I can say my father was always "there for me," even when he was not physically present, there can be breaks in dialogue and changes of rhythm. We all work in the grid world, but we can come in and out of our many dialogues.

Domestic Maintenance

Dialogue requires a maintenance budget—we cannot spend everything on the encounter. While the I-You encounter establishes its own place and time, dialogue veers in and out of the space-time of the absolute encounter, so it needs a place to be contained and protected. It is often best if this place cultivates and supports several kinds of encounters that work together to form dialogues. The same comforts that facilitate human dialogues can also inspire nonhuman encounters. This is why the domestic—however fraught—is a chief place for nonhuman dialogue.

The domestic support systems required by human dialogue are hidden, but nonhuman dialogue exposes them. Human speech, especially between friends, often seems effortless, weightless and placeless, in a word: easy. Dialogue with mute beings is different, it is troublesome, and for this reason the forces which sustain it are more conspicuous. Nowhere are dialogue's supports more visible than in the home, where the forces which sustain the domestic also create an atmosphere that encourages dialogues. In this book I avoid idealized, withdrawn, or aseptic concepts of the home, or any model where the family lives outside of time and politics. The desire to live outside of history, while perfectly understandable, is a trap.[34] Instead, I use a concept of the home drawn from Jewish political thought and psychoanalysis.[35] Seen as such, the home is set *within* politics and history, even as it develops a membrane to protect itself from them. Building and protecting this membrane provides dialogue with the space it requires.

What Lies Ahead

Chapter 1 explores the domestic spaces of dialogue, and the all-important work that goes into preserving and maintaining them. A Jewish notion of the domestic is developed as part of this process. Those interested in dialogue and not in Jewish Studies or theories of space should skip this chapter. Chapter 2 examines the general topic of dialogue with nonhuman animals, mainly to differentiate between human language and other sophisticated modes of communication. Chapter 3 focuses on the house cat (or a cat). The cat's anxiety reveals what, in the general sense, nonhuman dialogues can tell us about dialogue writ large. Chapter 4 digs into plant communication and the problems of dialogues with living beings that are very much unlike us, beings who are dispersed. Here, tempo and time are central. Chapter 5 delves into the nursery and explores the world of babies and the prelinguistic. Here, I draw heavily on Melanie Klein's work to try to understand crying and screaming. Chapter 6 crafts a theory of art and sensuality, seeking to show how dialogue can occur at the level of sensation. Finally, the conclusion asks questions about dialogue with the dying.

1

HOMES

Domesticity and Conflict

> Our couch is in a bower;
> Cedars are the beams of our house,
> Cypresses the rafters.
>
> —*Song of Songs*

> He who makes trouble for his household
> shall inherit the wind
>
> —*Proverbs*

THE EDIFICE OF TWENTIETH-CENTURY JEWISH THOUGHT HAS MANY chambers, and surely one of its most dazzling is the philosophy of relationships. But philosophy untempered by materialism tends to present relationships as placeless: They occur *between* men of good intention and similar income and seem to float above the world. There is a logic to this placelessness. From the perspective of someone in the midst of an encounter, the background does seem to recede; the location feels less important than the happening. But dialogue takes place over time and needs to be sustained even as we fade in and out of it. When we think about how to sustain dialogue place moves from the margins toward the center of our thinking. Some places are more conducive to dialogue than others; some places contain and shelter dialogues better than others.[1]

Relationships develop in specific places, not in an abstract space. In this chapter, I focus on one type of these places, the domestic. The domestic, at its best, encourages the happenings that support relationships and so plays an essential role in the day-to-day dialogues that sustain us. This includes nonhuman relationships; for example, most of our dialogues with animals involve domestic animals.

The domestic is often lazily thought of as an unimportant or castrated space, much as the domestic animal is considered an unimportant or castrated wild animal. If we think of the domestic as a substandard or less-real space or consider the term *domestication* to be as a slur, we impoverish our thinking about dialogue and how to cultivate it. Conversely, to valorize the domestic, as if it were intrinsically good, is to instrumentalize it, to turn it into a faddish weapon of the weak.

The domestic is a world where various beings develop with one another and is thus a space of uncanny activity, half-formed sexuality, aggression, and warmth. The following notion of the domestic space comes from multiple sources in modern Jewish thought, including Laura Levitt, Freud, and Melanie Klein. It is a notion deliberately hostile to the classical notions of house and home found in the political tradition that flows from Aristotle to John Rawls. My concern is not with any real Jewish home but rather with the home drawn from these sources. To give away the plot: The Aristotelian house is a nonpolitical space where nothing interesting occurs, whereas in the Jewish house, things happen: It is a place where fucked-up beings grow in proximity and relation to one another—a place of formation, protection, and care, but also of sex, violence, taboo, and rules.

To give dialogue a location allows us to ask how it can be cultivated (rather than viewing encounters as epiphanic moments that fall from the sky). To cultivate dialogue by cultivating spaces requires work, usually gendered—a crucial point in advancing discussion of domesticity, even animal domesticity.[2] It also requires us to think about scale. As Imhoff writes in "Homemaking in Palestine," some things exist or function only at certain scales; at the very least, some things occur with far greater ease and frequency at certain scales.[3] Dialogue tends to exist at small scales and is lost when you zoom out. The domestic encourages small-scale intimacy: From the becoming-sexual of a teenager, to the feeding of animals, to the eternal conflict with dirt and mold, to the muck and scent of the dying, the domestic is where long, drawn-out dialogues are given a place to occur.

The Domestic (Sphere) (in Arendt)

The home and its animals are not only marked off by their domesticity but also marked down. This discounted place serves propaganda as the "spirit" of politics—because politics and war, the serious business of men, are justified because these men are protecting the domestic, the grandmotherly space of scones, children, and ethics—but the domestic in-itself is rarely considered serious or vital.[4] This is a problem when it comes to thinking about relationships, which are more likely to develop in the kitchen than the agora or the boardroom.

Arendt's work is a good place to start when considering what role the house plays for both propagandists and classical philosophers. A conflicted theorist, Arendt uncovers the domestic space and its functions but seems to hold them in contempt. Like many of her generation, she was overwhelmed by nostalgia for the public square (be that in a commune, a kibbutz, or the agora), and although she sees the importance of the domestic, she frequently demeans it. This is unfortunate, as it results in a schema that treats Attic politics and its Aristotelian legacy with more esteem than they deserve.

Thus, Arendt says, "According to Greek thought, the human capacity for political organization is not only different from but stands in direct opposition to that natural association whose center is the home (oikoi) and the family."[5] This is presented crudely, and as being too crude, but it is nonetheless her starting point for thinking the domestic. This domestic is the space of the private, which lives in "the shadowy interior of the household."[6] So far, so simple: The public is the political, and the private is the domestic, and they are more or less opposites of each other. Things become complicated when the social is added, which is something of a middle term between the domestic and the political, with its own characteristics.[7]

Arendt tells a good story about the rise of the private space. It begins with the Romans, who "never sacrificed the private to the public, but . . . understood that these two realms could exist only in the form of coexistence." The story ends in the "modern age," where, enriched by the fruits of individualism, people use private spaces to make and cultivate things, some of which end up moving into the public world.[8] Interestingly, it does not occur to Arendt that the private could gain value not just by being opened to the masculine outside but also by placing more importance on the home's inhabitants (women, children, pets, servants, and slaves).[9] Instead, Arendt's story of the rise of the private ends with its near destruction by the same forces that elevated it to begin with: mass culture, mass bureaucracy, the decline of character, surveillance, and so on—social forces that are positioned against the domestic as a place of retreat.

Arendt's ideas provide significant insights into understanding the domestic space and its animals, but they are even more valuable for showing how the domestic is generally viewed and positioned by philosophy writ large. The domestic and the private are determined more by what they are *not* than by what they are. Despite Arendt's insistence that she does not devalue the private sphere, from the beginning to the end of her book, the private is deficient. Because the private is the not-political or not-public, it is marked by its deficiency and unreality. Perhaps more importantly, because the space is defined entirely by what it isn't, it is homogeneous.[10]

The political is a space of multiple interests: a plural world where different factions fight and negotiate for power, authority, and domination. The private is not part of this world, so it is a space of *unified* interests.[11] Because the house's interests are determined by daddy, it is assumed that the house is an extension of him, much as a tool is an extension of its user. Seen as such, the private is unified in its aims and organization; it has no public interests because it is the extension of an already existing interest (the father). Of course, this is nonsense. The domestic appears unified only when it is seen from the dizzying heights of political fantasy. This is why Freud is a preeminent Jewish thinker of the domestic: He presents the home as a space of the immanent uncanny, always aggressively and sexually divided against itself. This is why the *unheimlich* (lit. unhomelike) is so easily found in the home, perhaps in a bathroom mirror. In typical Germanic style, the home contains its own negative. To paraphrase filmmaker Alfred Hitchcock, Freud is to be thanked for putting violence back in the home, where it belongs.

Alternative Privacies

As Michael McKeon notes in his *Secret History of Domesticity*, while the distinction between the public and private is new, both categories and their differences are "a fundamental feature of traditional societies as well," no matter how one defines *traditional*.[12] The "difference" is that in traditional cultures, the differential relationship between public and private modes of experience is conceived as *a distinction that does not admit of separation*. In modernity, the public and the *private are separated out from each other*.[13]

With this in mind, we look for an alternate valuation of the domestic. Eva Mroczek describes a long tradition in Jewish thought of creating and protecting private or private-like spaces. Even a cursory reading of Elliot Wolfson's work demonstrates a long-standing concern with protected or secret spaces in kabbalah.[14] And the world of Genesis (a small world, by our standards) is an enclosure, protected from chaos and primeval waters; in this vein, the cliché that Genesis begins with a bet because the Torah is a house might actually have some validity.[15]

It is hardly the case that actual Jewish homes manage to escape the grip of the classical heritage and its repressions. Indeed, as Dworkin notes, there are elements of the tradition explicitly committed to the antipolitical home as a form of prison: "Right-wing Judaism and right-wing Christianity both guarantee that women will continue to have a place outside history but inside the home: through childbearing. Without that, women know they have nothing."[16] The domestic, no matter how it's theorized, can be a trap.[17] The liberal-classical home claims to offer protection for women and children in exchange for removing them from the political sphere. A quick look at murder statistics confirms that this apparent protection often turns into predation.[18] Levitt's work, more political-theological than commonly supposed, presents the classical-liberal house as an attempt to establish a "whole" through pseudoconsensual domination.[19] Here, we see clear echoes of the domestic-as-unity, where women "freely" trade their freedom in exchange for the home's supposed protections.

The Jewish model is not freer, but it provides a better model for thinking about domesticity. This, however, only if we avoid any nostalgia for the "Jewish home," a home presumably haunted by the scent of freshly baked goods, old books, and gender oppression. This is not an attempt to use tradition to resist capital or to sneak in orthodoxy under the guise of emancipation. Instead, I am interested in an understanding of the domestic that shows how it encourages dialogues among the strange beings forced together in the home. It is hardly true that Rabbinic Judaism valorizes the household; the Talmud frequently denigrates the feminine domestic. The woman and the house are often identified with each other ("just as a house has doors, so the woman has doors," etc.), and although they are not reduced to tools for Aristotle's "head of the household," nonetheless, "the husband has exclusive rights to his 'house,' to his wife's reproductive capacity, but not vice versa."[20] This asymmetry is to be expected, as are its contemporary echoes, as when Levinas writes in a Talmudic reading that "'woman' is the space 'man' inhabits."[21] We should not be fooled into thinking that by exploring the Jewish tradition, we are escaping patriarchy. But we do get a different *kind* of patriarchy and, in turn, a different (and better) concept of the domestic. In rabbinic thought, the domestic is (forgive the term) troubled and not merely a privation of the public.

Despite the rabbinic disposition to hermeneutically subdue and enervate biblical women, the house appears in the Talmud as a site of conflict—one that mirrors the temple, a virtual strife-ridden location: "Destabilizing the Temple and its priesthood served as a literary ploy of sorts to confront real-life instability and human frailty centered, as it often is, on the household."[22] This instability is superior to Aristotle's fantasy of a house where all the occupants are mere tools for the owner; as in the rabbinic house/temple, *things happen*.

The relationship between the house and law is inverted. As Meirav Jones notes, the Jewish house is a place of law and prohibition; it is not a question of imposing "external" laws into the house; rather, law emanates from the house (as seen in the case of the *eruv*, the near-invisible boundary that allows Orthodox Jews to carry things on Shabbes by extending the boundaries of the house into the public sphere).[23] The Jewish home is thus a place of regulation, but it is a notoriously unstable regulation. In Freud, it is the birthplace of fundamental regulatory principles (rules about sex and violence), but these rules are constantly being transformed and transgressed.

Any theory that describes the house as *only* a place of warmth is of little value. This is seen when Rosenzweig uses the domestic to re-create Aristotelian unity while also desiring a contained equality.[24] In his maudlin claim "the chamber of the Jewish heart is the home," we see a place where certain things and relationships are possible, but only at the cost of work and action. Levinas sharpens this distinction: The external world is the masculine world of hard reason and is not habitable.[25] The feminine home provides warmth and a "moral paradigm," and it is here women fulfill their spiritual purpose: enabling men to go out and function in the public world.[26]

A more usable concept of the domestic can be found in Buber and Heschel, which places less emphasis on gender and more on what can happen *only* in a domestic or private place. As Carson notes, despite Heschel's seeming bias toward time as the essence of Jewish life, the domestic plays an essential role.[27] If Judaism focuses on creating buildings in time—the Sabbath being a prime example of giving time a rhythm as well as a form—this time and the things constructed within it also need a space, a domestic one.[28] The private is not a space of privation but a space where life can be protected as it unfolds and transforms.

Protection is fraught: Those who offer protection are often the very people we need to be protected from. The domestic is no exception.[29] But without a barrier to protect our becoming and our developing relationships—without a protected space where relationships might develop—life and dialogue become extremely difficult, if not impossible. It is not surprising that the formation of protective barriers is thus of utmost concern for psychoanalytic theorists of the domestic. Freud goes so far as to claim that these barriers are intrinsic to all living beings:

> This tiny piece of living matter floats around in an external world charged with energies . . . and would be destroyed by their stimulative effect if it were not equipped with some form of protection against stimulation. It acquires this protection by virtue of the fact that its outermost surface abandons the structure proper to living things, becomes to all intents and purposes inorganic, and in consequence operates as a special covering or membrane impeding the stimuli. . . . The outer layer becomes necrotic—but by doing so it protects all the deeper-lying ones from suffering a similar fate. . . . For the living organism, the process protecting it against stimuli is almost more important than the process whereby it receives stimuli.[30]

As fanciful as this interpretation is, where each organism forms its own little house composed of its own dead matter, it demonstrates Freud's commitment to dynamic modes of protection and an understanding of their importance. It is an antidote to macho demands that we live authentic and unprotected lives: to claim that the exposed life is the genuine life is cruel and usually hypocritical.[31] But more to the point, Freud here describes essential human behaviors, even if his biological theory cannot be extended as far as Freud might wish.

Primo Levi seems to test Freud's theory while playing his part in Auschwitz's "gigantic biological and social experiment." He comes to similar conclusions about the human ability to extrude a shelter: "Man's capacity to dig himself in, to secrete a shell, to build around himself a tenuous barrier of defense, even in apparently desperate circumstances, is astonishing and merits serious study. It is based on an invaluable activity of adaptation, partly passive and unconscious, partly active: hammering a nail above his bunk to hang up his shoes; concluding tacit pacts of non-aggression with neighbors; understanding and accepting the customs and laws of a single *Kommando*, a single *Block*. One has made oneself a nest; the trauma of transplantation is over."[32]

With a nail to hold our shoes and agreements with our neighbors, we have the beginnings of a shelter. No one would call this domestic, but this drive and process, when allowed to be carried to perfection or completion, is the basis for a domestic space. This is another instance of the Jewish domestic as something that is extruded by, or emanates from, developing *organisms*, rather than something that is a partitioning off by a political *agent*. In the former, the domestic house and its formation is an activity; in the latter, it is a zone created by a person who wants a break from activity (namely, politics).

The shells we secrete can be formed into functional, domestic shelters, but neither this process nor its results are necessarily restful. This element of unrest is often missing from Buber's overly folkish descriptions of them. This is because he focuses more on emphasizing relationships than on the space where they occur. Buber rotates vertical relationships (such as those between people and God, or a plea to the heavens above) ninety degrees; once rotated, the religious relationship is understood not as pointing upward to a distant deity but as existing between us, as relationships and dialogues between creatures.[33] When Buber is done with them, theological relationships are horizontal, covering the earth instead of reaching to the heavens.[34]

That these relations can sometimes seem unreal is a consequence of Buber's effort to defend them against the grid, to defend dialogue against universal measurement and discourse.[35] Buber's life's work is an attempt to defend creaturely life from a world where everything is placed on a coordinate system, where everything has its place. But sometimes, he goes too far, and the mere fact that something has a place suggests to him that it is part of the grid world and not a full relationship: "And even as prayer is not in time but time in prayer, the sacrifice not in space but space in the sacrifice—and whoever reverses the relation annuls the reality—I do not find the human being to whom I say You in any Sometime and Somewhere."[36]

This is clear enough: When my daughter and I are in dialogue, space is transformed and occurs within the relationship; the relationship comes first; and the space is its consequence. In this absolute separation from universal space, Buber seeks to sustain an absolute distinction between different types of relationships.

But is it completely true that space is a consequence of the situation? The statement "I do not find the human being to whom I say You in any Sometime and Somewhere" works in an abstract sense, but taken in its basic sense, the statement is also plainly false. I am far more likely to say "You" to my daughter at 770 Johnson Street than I am in a parking lot.

My home, while located sometime and somewhere, cultivates and encourages relationships.[37] The same can be true of a store, a bar, or a hair salon: Some spaces encourage relationships more than others. Buber's students spend very little time asking what *sort* of spaces encourage relationships, and even less on how these spaces are built, maintained, cleaned, and sustained.[38] This is unfortunate, as the Jewish textual tradition provides countless resources for thinking about these protective spaces.[39] Indeed, when Buber comes closest to thinking about these protective bubbles, he tends to draw from Hasidic sources.

To develop Buber's ideas, we must consider the creation and maintenance of spaces that encourage dialogue—private spaces that are withdrawn. In a time when access and connection are treated as ends in themselves, thought demands disconnection and exclusion. The domestic has a role to play here, provided we think of it not as a place of eternal peace and unity but as one of conflict and sexuality as well as calm and goofiness. For this to happen, modern Jewish thought is, or should be, informed by two extraordinary thinkers: Freud and Klein.

Which thinkers have done more to demonstrate that we are fundamentally composed of relationships?[40] Or that the supposedly peaceful world of the domus is shot through with sex and conflict? By noting the simple fact that our sexuality and aggression *develop* in a domestic world—and so the *objects* of our aggressive and sexual fantasies are likely to be domestic fellow travelers—Freud and Klein have both repelled and educated several generations of thinkers. When Freud switched the emphasis from the father (who "runs" the house like a collection of tools he owns) to the son (who develops as a political and sexual being within the house), the fantasy of a peaceful and unified private space evaporated.[41] From there, the house is, as it were, split open: not to reveal its contents to the public but rather just to be seen—even by itself—as a zone of immanent conflict.

This attentiveness to domestic conflict is a theoretical move as important as it is obvious: The anxiety Freud still causes is surely in part due to this exposure of the dark side of the house (as filmmaker David Lynch does with seemingly quaint communities, or Hitchcock with the haute bourgeois). The quiet immanent conflicts of the domestic, the sexual undercurrents, the competition between competing interests, are obvious to anyone who has ever lived in a home.

Any conceptual repair of the domestic will proceed not despite but because of the many imperfections and conflicts the home is riven with. But such a rehabilitation must also acknowledge that the house is—or should be—a space of protection from the elements, the political, work, and capital. The domestic is an ambivalent space (what space isn't?), offering both protection and violence; it shelters us from the very thing it enables, but it remains a shelter nonetheless. Diverse interests play at equality over a meal but undermine each other with gossip worthy of Marquise de Merteuil; it is a space of confused sexuality but also a place of protection from the rapacious violence of the street. It is every bit as interesting as the political. It is a space that, at its best, encourages and sustains many silent dialogues and, at its worst, can damage a person so thoroughly that they will never again be capable of intimate language. It's also where my cat lives.[42]

Foundational Relationships, with a Soupçon of Ethics

For Buber, the home is not an evasion of the nonhuman but a space where relations to nonhumans emerge. In his work on Hasidism and on Pu Songling's *Strange Tales from Liaozhai*, Buber is interested in nonhuman entities that populate the home. This is why he claims to have been drawn to Pu Songling's work:

> What attracted me was something I did not find so fully expressed in similar tales of any other people: an air of intimacy and harmony. Here demons are . . . beings of our own world, merely arising from a deeper, darker region. . . . Here the order of nature is not ruptured but extended; nothing interferes with the plenitude of life, and everything living carries the seed of the ghostly. The demonic blossoms not only in animals, plants, and rocks, but strives to compact into human form as in a fruit: . . . every act bears witness to a demon who, as your friend, as your wife, as your son, enters your house and rewards you. Yet none of this is uncanny: it is home, it is life.[43]

The home is identified as a region that (like the ghosts and foxes themselves) is not cut off from "life." When people speak of the "real world" as compared to the home, they generally mean only the world's most violent and alienating spaces. That both are part of *the* world escapes them.

Most striking is Buber's identification of *Tales*' domestic intimacy: The home is not an escape from real life. This has an interesting consequence: The *Tales* are singular in their refusal to mystify relationships with "spiritual" beings, as strange creatures, foxes, ghosts, and animated objects can become part of the household (and, indeed, the civil service). This is taken well into the realm of sex, as the *Tales* are splendidly carnal, and sex with spiritual beings is commonplace.[44] Buber's reading of the *Tales* is informed by his work with Hasidic tales, but while his image of the Hasidic home is nostalgic and "mystified," the home of the *Strange Tales* is far more chaotic and erotic, and it comes closer to the work of Klein and Freud than a pious depiction of Lublin found in a Hasidic story. If we use one volume to open the other and correct Buber's reading of the Hasidic tales with his reading of the *Strange Tales*, what do we see? The domestic is the space where we first encounter nonhumans with love.[45] Less dramatically, Buber writes, "I find ... our relationship to the domestic animals with whom we live, and even that to the plants in our gardens, is properly included as the lowest floor of the ethical building. The Hasidim even see it as beginning with the implements of work."[46] The lowest floor may not be the most exciting, but it is foundational; it is a place where nonhuman dialogue begins. Unfortunately, Buber never really explains *why* the domestic is a fertile space for dialogue.

From the avuncular to the paternal, the queer enclave or the hippie commune, what all of these domestic spaces share, even the most antiseptic suburban monument to fear, is that countless creatures dwell in them. But of these creatures, only a few really enter our dialogical space. Granted, some of us may speak with spiders, but who has had regular conversations with silverfish? One should not too blithely embrace our involvement with companion species. Yes, my skin is covered with bugs, but I don't notice or care about them. My house was "home" to many stray children, especially those with artistic inclinations. My mother adopted them, the walls adopted mice, the chimney adopted bats, and so on, but the full members of the household—meaning those able to speak and be heard—were the humans and the pets.

This may be good, it may be bad, but it's how the domestic works: It is a selectively permeable space, not an open one. Slaughtering moths without a thought, we plant flowers for monarchs in our front yards. Culture and location determine which animals are allowed in: Dialogically speaking, "wild" animals are merely animals you don't usually encounter. A friend of mine grew up in a swarm, surrounded by birds (literally hundreds of them), and had a goat for a pet. I can barely imagine this, and it sounds horrifying to me. One person's wilderness is another person's house. We wake in an unseen swarm, but alongside only a few.

2

ANIMALS

Communication and Language

> How can it be that a man who did not know the mind of his animal could have known the mind of the most high?
>
> —*Avodah Zarah 4a*

WHAT DOES BUBER MEAN WHEN HE SAYS THAT we can dialogue with creatures who cannot speak?[1] Typically, dialogue is a certain use of language, a *type* of talking, so how is it possible without speech? To understand this, we'll look at our relationships with animals, what Buber calls the "threshold" of language: "Here the relationship vibrates in the dark and remains below language."[2] It's a good place to start because many of us already have language-like relationships with animals. After exploring the hopelessly broad notion of *animal* we will move on to domestic animals and eventually trade them in for the even more specific *Felis catus* (house cat).

There is a gap between humans and nonhuman animals. This gap and what it means pose a serious difficulty, one that many theorists try to overcome by fiat. Despite our desire to emphasize our overlapping lives, the chasms between humans and nonhumans remain, and no effusive prose can change this. The most noticeable of these gaps is language. Unsupported by language, animal dialogues face complications that rarely affect human relations. When ensuring that both conversants are on the same page, that we are not projecting our thoughts and feelings onto our partner, animal dialogue presents different dilemmas than human conversation does. Although these difficulties may bedevil practice, they are an asset for theory: It's easier to think about something when its cracks are showing. Spoken language makes dialogue easy, and when things are easy and straightforward, why think about them? The ability to do things with words, to treat words as things, is an extraordinary power. But speech, because it is facile, obscures its own conditions.

Specifically, language obscures how tenuous dialogue is. A human conversation seems to stand on its own, as if the words we speak continue to exist independently of the dialogue itself. In a sense, they do. I can talk to you, the conversation is evanescent, we "communicate," and we move on. But the words remain, at least in theory, because they can be written down, transcribed. It's perhaps too grand to compare a transcription to a musical composition, but once I've said my words, they can be repeated, reperformed, or read. Like a performance, the vanishing conversation is endlessly repeatable and, therefore, *in theory* not really evanescent at all. In principle, a conversation's "data" can live on even as we rot. Conversations feel stable because the words can be repeated.[3] But this stability can be deceptive, suggesting a security that is not there and a mutuality that might not exist.[4]

What does this mean? Let's preview Buber's cat passage, which has been echoed and parodied throughout modern Jewish philosophy. *After* a description of encountering his cat, Buber discusses the emotions that end his animal encounter:

> There the glance of the animal, the language of anxiety, had risen hugely—and set almost at once....
>
> It is for the sake of the language of this barely perceptible rising and setting of the spirit sun that I relate this minute occurrence that happened to me more than once. No other event has made me so deeply aware of the evanescent actuality in all relationships to other beings, the sublime melancholy of our lot, the fated lapse into It of every single You.[5]

This "melancholy" has frustrated Buber interpreters who see him as a prophet of an unending day, but the anxiety is rarely noted. What is the anxiety? It is the recognition of evanescence: All encounters are extremely fragile and *contain their own end*, much as life contains death within its concept.

It is an animal who teaches Buber that all encounters are fleeting precisely because animals don't speak. Cats can signal us, but they don't use symbols, which means our dialogue is driven by bodies. It is like a soap bubble, waiting to pop. The fragility of encounter is less obvious where humans are concerned because our language provides an artificial stability.

Animal dialogue is unanchored by words, and this emphasizes its support and maintenance systems. Thus, at the boundary of human being, where we look beyond the edge of language, the fragility of all dialogue is evident. This might explain why many of the people I've known who spend most of their time speaking with tools and animals are painfully aware of the brittleness of human sociality.

Are We Sure That Animals Don't Use Language?

The powers of language, written and spoken, have made irresistible the claim that it is the source of human greatness and animal insignificance.[6] Those who wished to save some dignity for nonhumans have often declared that animals have their own languages; we just cannot understand them. From the Sufi *The Case of Animals versus Man* to the Hasidic "Language of the Birds," we find the compelling idea that nonhumans use language as rich and referential as our own. While cognitive ethology has provided some much-needed nuance here—animals do communicate with an extraordinary richness and scope of feeling—the line seems to hold: Most humans use language, and other animals don't.[7]

Nonhumans communicate in great detail, but they lack the self-reference, arbitrariness, infinities, and paradoxes of language. As Deacon notes, "We alone brood about what didn't happen, and spend a large part of each day musing about the way things could have been if events had transpired differently. And we alone ponder what it will be like not to be."[8] With language, we begin to understand concrete notions of nothingness, self-reference, and boundlessness. While the importance of these concepts is open to doubt, their inherence in language seems less doubtful.

The question of animal language is tied to moral, political, and perhaps even religious concerns. It is (for good reason) an emotional issue, so emotions are often substituted for arguments. Supporters of animal language are hardly the only ones to use evocation to move their audience; those who deny animal language, or those who go so far as to deny animal cognition, often rely on a cold reason, which is just as emotionally manipulative (perhaps more so).[9]

Many texts that claim animals have language challenge the idea of human exceptionalism (which is good), but they do so by insinuating that anyone who thinks differently does so out of fear (which is bad).[10] If this appeal doesn't work, we often encounter an ethical argument and a cognitive argument. The ethical argument states that granting animals language would be "empowering" for them.[11] Supposedly, if we think that animals have language, we would be less likely to kill and exploit them. This is odd. Humans have shown little to no compunction about killing and exploiting each other. A better argument might be that we shouldn't inflict unnecessary pain on any creature, whether they are loquacious or not.

The cognitive argument is more sympathetic. Historically, many philosophers who deny animals language have also denied them thought. This is patently ridiculous: Animals think, feel, plan, mourn, read desires on each other's faces, and so on.[12] Those who defend animal dignity argue that therefore they have language (and so, in turn, thought). Again, I'd reverse this: The fact that animals do not use language doesn't suggest they don't think; rather, it suggests a great deal of thinking takes place without language. The more we study nonhumans—and ourselves—the more this seems to be the case.

Finally, there is something comforting about placing humans back among our animal kin. Erasing the line between "us" and "them" seems not only ethically desirable but also soothing. However, the chasms that divide us are not merely a fantasy of human arrogance, and, further, there is little reason to think that removing a human-animal difference will lead to better behavior. Many advances of the last several centuries have involved removing humans from the throne and returning us to a material world. But this has not stopped us from alienating ourselves and destroying ecosystems through extractive practices and politics—just the opposite is true. The chasms of language and technological organization remain open, and it is too late to pretend otherwise.

Animal Communications: A Peircean Aside

The following short section discusses some abstruse American philosophy. I hope this clarifies *how* some nonhumans communicate and how this differs from human language. These concepts may clarify the rest of the book, but they are not essential. Therefore, those with no interest in these ideas should skip to the next section ("I'm Not a Mind Reader").

The difficulty with the "other animals can talk" thesis is that they can't. So far, humans are the only animals we know of who use language. Those who argue otherwise tend to confuse communication and language, or they have a hopelessly vague notion of what language is. I say hopelessly vague, and not vague, because all definitions of language are beset by ambiguities.

Communication and language are not the same. A traffic light communicates, but it is not using language. Weeping communicates even more, but it is also not language. The reverse is also true: I can use language and not communicate. Many scholars of animal behavior are unbothered by this distinction or those among different types of signs. Thus, we often see something like "It's my contention that those [animal] communication systems can be considered 'language.'" The question of animals and language is thereby reduced to one of information and meaning: Do animal communications transmit information? Do signs mean something to the animals that use them? Most of us would likely answer yes to both questions. But this does not mean that animals use language. There is a difference between language and other ways of communicating information. So we must ask again: are animal signs and signals language?

To be clear, if we consider all communication language, then animals have language—but this renders the word *language* useless. There is a qualitative difference between human and nonhuman communication systems. Terrence Deacon (via C. S. Peirce) explains this difference by invoking different *types* of signs: Humans and animals both use indexical signs, but so far as we know, only humans use symbols. There is thus a qualitative difference between human and nonhuman communication systems. The following section briefly explores this difference.

With Peirce, we can divide signs into three large groups: icons, indexes, and symbols.[13] The details are unimportant; what matters is that icons have one relationship, indexes have two, and symbols have three. For the moment I am mostly concerned with the last two Indexes are symbols that are in some way connected to the thing they are about. Smoke indexes fire. Jiggling the food bowl indicates dinner. "A thermometer indicates the temperature of water, a weathervane indicates the direction of the wind, and a disagreeable odor might indicate the presence of a skunk."[14] Incredibly complex and deep communication can be built out of indexes, such as bees "dancing" to indicate a location, or weeping, which indexes grief. In each case, the index, which has two terms, functions as a relationship between the sign and its object. The index directs us to whatever it is about.

Peirce says the following about thm "*The index asserts nothing*; it only says 'There!' It takes hold of our eyes, as it were, and forcibly directs them to a particular object, and there it stops. Demonstrative and relative pronouns are nearly pure indices, because they denote things without describing them; so are the letters on a geometrical diagram, and the subscript numbers which in algebra distinguish one value from another without saying what those values are."[15]

Indexes can do a great deal of cognitive and emotional work; they are not simple and can be combined to transmit far more data than your average symbol. Body language can often tell us more than words and is almost entirely indexical. However, the index itself, the sign itself, indicates only what it is about. It points at a signified, nothing more (and nothing less).

I believe animals are at home in the world of indexes: calls, signals, symptoms, indications, coloring, selves, and others. All of these indexes in some sense "bottom out," or refer to, a thing in the world, be it an object, a behavior, a feeling, or a process. There can be interactions between signs (different calls mean things in different places, or in the context of other signs), but they end in the world. Each sign has a sort of rope that connects it to a thing it is about. And this is the difference between indexes and symbols, between our communication and that of other animals: Symbols have three relationships, and one of these is (or can be) an arbitrary relationship to another sign or a general idea. One symbol can interpret another, and this in turn another. Symbols are not necessarily attached to anything real; they are more like webs than ropes.

This difference is easily obscured because the same sign can be an index or a symbol—it depends on context. For example, the word *blue* has an arbitrary relationship with the color: The word itself isn't blue (you're probably reading it in black and white), and you would only know that it is connected to the color if someone taught you that. Language is full of arbitrary relationships, but so is signaling. A red light only means "stop" because you've been taught that. I assume that several nonhuman animals could be taught to identify the word *blue* with the color. Whenever I say *blue*, the creature points at the color. We might then say the animal has learned the word—and in a sense it has, but only as an index. It is still part of a set of *signals*: It knows what the word refers to, but it cannot necessarily use it as part of a language.

Let's take the same word and view it as a symbol. Like indexes, symbols often have arbitrary relationships to their objects, but they have another relationship that connects to another symbol by way of an interpretant.[16] I can teach you what the word *blue* means exclusively through other words: "The color blue is that of a clear sky." I can also (and this is extremely important) *translate* it. *Azul* is connected to the same color, but by a different (Spanish) web of symbols and minds; the same is true for the Hebrew כָּחֹל

and so on. I can take the word *blue*, transcribe it, translate it, and give it to another person. Further, I can take the word *blue* as an object and talk about it (how it sounds, the letters that form it, its history and usage, and so on). This network of communications is almost explosive because it can expand infinitely in any direction and has countless potential connections. This is why there are no simple languages, and why teaching a dog to identify twenty words is not the same thing as teaching it language. Not because there is a quantitative difference between that and the twenty thousand words humans probably know, but because humans can use those words in a qualitatively different manner.

Animal communication is thus not a degenerate or incomplete form of human language—it's just different. Animal signal systems routinely exceed those of humans in terms of complexity and use media and have objects we cannot even sense, let alone communicate. Many people who want to elevate animals by granting them language end up diminishing them because the language they are left with is a poor thing.[17] Animal communication is different, not worse.

Finally, this distinction between human language and animal communication does not disconnect us from the rest of the natural world. Some, like Slobodchikoff, complain, "An unbridgeable gap between us and the rest of life just doesn't make sense. After all, every other system in humans has its roots in other species, and can often be traced up the evolutionary line."[18] But unbridgeable gaps, or qualitative differences, happen all the time, just like cooling water transforms into ice. The complexity of the eye was used to support creationism, as it appeared to show such a profound qualitative difference that it seemed inconceivable for it to have developed in steps. However, with research and patience, these steps were found. Human language is connected to the communication systems of other animals and is also qualitatively different: Symbols are built on indexes, which in turn depend on icons. Each level emerges from the previous but cannot be reduced to it. This means that although our brains and bodies are largely continuous with nonhumans, there is a "singular discontinuity between human and nonhuman minds, or to be more precise, between brains that use this form of communication and brains that do not."[19] Again, this is not to claim superiority, but difference. Triadic signs can be completely detached from a dialogue and then reproduced or translated. This translatability and reproducibility give language an unearned sense of robustness, which in turn hides the dialogical situation from us.

I'm Not a Mind Reader

"What is it *like* to talk to an animal?"[20] This is a narrow question that helps us focus on what is familiar to us—our part in a dialogue. What might be lost in scope I hope to regain in security, even as I address the braver souls who have inquired into what's going on for the animal. This allows us to address the *effects* of our dialogue: what is gained and what is lost by an attentive insecurity.[21]

Buber says we can dialogue with animals, but in what sense? I admit at the outset that computer-bound people like me find talking to nonhumans difficult. This is perhaps why so many books have emerged seeking to thematize "natural" relationships. I have no interest in damning a genre, but these books are often heavy on anecdote, saturated with adjectives, and short on theory. One of the better texts in this class—Svendson's *Understanding Animals*—which unabashedly focuses on pets, is useful because he articulates a common understanding of how we talk to animals. In a nutshell, he makes talking with pets too easy and thus obscures the real difficulties with animal dialogues (difficulties that are precisely why they are philosophically intriguing). Svendson writes, "I have never interacted with an animal that did not speak. . . . When I have encountered animals that I have tried to understand, they have spoken without exception, but of course it is me who has spoken for them. When I have tried to understand what is happening in the animal's consciousness, I have been unable to avoid articulating this understanding linguistically, as if it were the animal itself that spoke. I too am speaking to the animals."[22]

The honesty expressed in the above passage recommends it. Svendson speaks for the animal in human language, and because he thinks the animal's thoughts in human language, he unabashedly leaps over the difference between him and his interlocutor by "translating" the animal's communications into human language. This is, of course, projection, but one could argue that we do this with other human beings too.

This position ignores essential difficulties. Svendson justifies this by claiming that animals communicate both within and across species, which is true. The questionable aspect arises when Svendson uses a "very broad concept of language," which allows him (in this example) to say that language equals communication.[23] Animal communication is read in terms of human language *because the animal's thoughts are "read" in human language*. This is part of a series of errors identified by Kristen Andrews, a thoughtful critic of "mind reading."

Mind reading does not mean the magic ability to see people's thoughts but rather the ability to know what someone is thinking based on their words or actions. Two important questions arise: Can we read animal minds in this way? Do animals read each other's minds, or our minds, in this way? There is a justifiable temptation to answer yes. I know what an animal is thinking by watching their behavior, and vice versa. Through this mutual mind reading, we develop a shared folk psychology that allows us to attribute thoughts across species.[24] If we accept that we read each other's minds, then Svendson's position makes sense; he thinks in language, so he reads an animal's thoughts the same way.

Kristen Andrews argues for a more critical position, which I also embrace. Folk psychology, both ours and that of other animals, is not founded on mind reading. *Because we don't read "minds," we read people.* The "mind" is an extra, and unneeded, step. Andrews writes, "We would not look at that person and think: 'A person writhing and screaming like that would usually be in a state of pain, so there is good reason to assume that the person I am now looking at is feeling pain.' We would carry out no such deduction, but rather see the pain from the person's behavior. We are even less likely to think: 'I cannot know if he's in pain, because his feelings are just something that exists within him, beyond what I can recognize.'"[25]

Pain is a good example because pain recognition is shared across species, hence Bentham's famous claim: "The question is not, Can they reason?, nor Can they talk? but, Can they suffer?"[26] If you cry out in pain, I don't think "that cry suggests they are feeling pain" or, worse, that "that cry of pain means their mind is occupied with pain." I simply see you in pain. Attributing this pain to some other force or substance (like your mind) is almost certainly done after the fact.

Svendson's translation of animal feeling into human language is thus not a problem because it's anthropocentric: It's a problem because it misunderstands how we relate to animals (and each other) by overstressing the importance of thought. Kristen Andrews's work is germane not for her antirepresentational stance or her claim that regarding communication, predictions are more important than propositions (although I think these are both true and useful points to remember when we engage in animal dialogues).[27] Rather, I rely on her demonstration of the quasiphenomenological position that we (and many other animals) read people, not minds. Andrews's shift away from propositional mental contents better reflects the way we relate to other people. This leads to an odd situation: the seemingly romantic claim that animals use language *over*-values human cognition and so impedes our ability to talk with animals.

Treating others as person-like requires not understanding, but attentiveness and perception. Hence, Andrews and others have shown that reading animals does not need linguistic communication. But instead of eliminating our difficulties, this only increases them. As noted in the introduction, Buber considers animals to be at the threshold of language. "Threshold" relationships are *processed* by us in a language-like manner. However, we should not be misled by the language-like nature of our animal relationships into thinking they consist of some special kind of language, however deficient. These relationships must be understood on their own terms: Yes, one member is a language user (us), so language might pervade the relationship, but it does not constitute it.

The Animal Threshold

When Buber published *I and Thou* in 1923, he unwittingly presented all encounters with nature as being essentially the same. The animal is situated in a subsection of nature, and nature is in turn at the threshold of language.[28] But we need to delineate many more subsections before Buber's animal dialogues can be useful. He came to realize this, and in a 1957 addendum to *I and Thou* he wrote "Instead of considering nature as a single whole, as we usually do, we must consider its different realms separately."[29] Indeed. At the very least, we must separate animals from the rest of nature, although we will soon find that this Aristotelian division is still not enough—there is a massive distance between a conversation with a spider and one with a deer, between a domestic animal and a wild one. So, how can we divide "nature" to better understand animal dialogues?

Simondon presents the construction of "Western" human/animal differentiations as a historical process. The first, pre-Socratic, distinctions were not connected to the intellect but to movement and vitality. There, the big difference is not between humans and nonhumans but between creatures that can move and those that cannot. "It is a relatively recent idea to contrast animal and human life, and to see human functions as fundamentally different from animal functions."[30] In the ethical Socrates, Simondon finds evidence of one of the earliest doctrines where humans are incomparably different from other natural beings.[31] This line in the sand is then drawn in more durable matter by the post-Socratics.

If we tell the story this way, "what comes out of the teachings of Antiquity is that what occurs in man and what occurs in animals is comparable.... Not identical but comparable."[32] I leave the accuracy of Simondon's details to historians, but this is the picture inherited by the modern philosophers who in turn inform Buber's concept of the animal. Simondon's story, like most such stories, is one of conflicts, and it ends with the enlightenment opposition to Montaigne, the last representative of a tradition where humans and animals share essential characteristics.[33] For Montaigne, animals and humans share not only vitality but also *psychology*: Both animals and humans think, feel, and are driven by similar instincts. For Simondon, "Montaigne's intentions are quite clear: . . . He wants to humiliate human pride, because the human pride for theories too systematic in nature is what leads to us burning men, to religious wars. . . . Thus one has to reintegrate man into the order of Creation, make it so that he conceives of himself as being a close relative to animals who live in an ordered manner."[34] Montaigne serves Simondon as a foil to the Great Monster in all of these stories: Descartes.

Descartes's move is radical, not because he draws a line between human and animal life but because of *the way* he draws the line: The line is no longer between reason and instinct. For Descartes, animals *are no longer instinctual*; instinct involves too much feeling, desire, and psychology. Instead of being instinctual, animals are now *mechanical*; they are automatons.[35] As Jessica Riskin notes, we must be careful when discussing automatons because, for many "enlighteners," the automaton was a vital being.[36] But despite attempts to reclaim the automaton—and also Descartes—apologetic readings miss the point regarding Descartes's animal. It is an automaton of pure extension, a machine in the most banal sense of the word. As Berger notes, Descartes's identification of the animal as machine is connected to the use of animals as machines. Before cars, we used horses, and even today, we measure engines in horsepower.[37]

Descartes is a little too cruel, but his theory finds a dark and humorous echo in what is perhaps the funniest work of modern Jewish thought, Maimon's *Autobiography*:

> It so happened that a goat was lying in our path. I hit the goat several times with my walking stick; in response, my friends accused me of brutality. I shot back: "What is brutality? Do you think that the goat feels pain when I beat it with my stick? You are quite wrong. According to Sturm, who was a Cartesian, the goat is merely a machine."

My friends laughed heartily and said: "Can't you hear the goat crying out when you beat it?" I replied: "Yes, of course, it makes noise, but when I beat a drum, it does, too."

This answer astonished my friends, and soon the whole city had learned that my mind had gone soft, for I had argued that a goat was a drum.[38]

In the form of dark humor we see one ramification of Descartes making humans and animals into different kinds of things. This view softened over the following century, but even Kant's seemingly different theory of animals is drawn from Descartes. For Kant, the distinction between us and animals is not that we are more reasonable or less instinctual; rather, it is that we are free and animals are not.[39] But in nontechnical parlance, the mechanical *is* the unfree. Mechanisms, in this standard sense, do not want things but merely do things; even the bare amount of desire required for doing comes from the user, not the machine. So Descartes's treatment of the animal-machine lives on in Kant's understanding of animals as unfree.

Even stranger, Kant considers the notion of freedom to be inborn. In a rather bizarre passage, Kant writes, "Even the child who has just wrenched itself from the mother's womb seems to enter the world with loud cries, unlike all other animals, simply because it regards the inability to make use of its limbs as constraint, and thus it immediately announces its claim to freedom (a representation that no other animal has)."[40]

The phrase *unlike all the other animals* is as bizarre as anything Aristotle ever wrote and as easily disproven. Yet Kant distinguishes the very first sounds a human makes from the animal world, not because the animal is a machine but because it has no relationship to freedom or its representations.

Kant's *Anthropology* rewards readers with several similar passages where the human is separated from the other animals by a wall of freedom. For almost every such passage we find a corresponding text in Montaigne, whose goal is to not only bring humans down to the level of other creatures (as per Simondon) but also lift human reason into the world of life, where reason runs aground and we are better off helping than judging. "Infant cries are common to most other animals; nearly all can be seen wailing and whining long after they are born; such behaviour is quite appropriate to the helplessness that they feel. As for eating, it is natural to us and to them; it does not have to be learned."[41]

For Montaigne, it is not knowledge that is innate, but metabolism and helplessness. We enter the world hungry and crying, and this fragility is shared with other animals.

While Montaigne sees human thought as an evasion of creaturely life, Kant sees it as a complete break with animality:

> The faculty of intuition (pure or empirical) contains only the singularity of objects, whereas the faculty of concepts contains the universality of representations, the rule to which the manifold of sensuous intuitions must be subordinated in order to bring unity to the cognition of the object.—*Therefore understanding certainly is of higher rank than sensibility, with which irrational animals can manage provisionally, following implanted instincts, like a people without a sovereign. But a sovereign without a people (like understanding without sensibility) is not able to do anything at all.*[42]

Here Kant's use of political models to explain human cognition and action (most notably, his preoccupation with autonomy) reaches bizarre heights, and nowhere is his distance from Buber clearer. Kant believes that animals don't have understanding because they can't categorize singulars under universals: this means they see individual things and people (singulars), but they form no general ideas about them. They have no *I*, no freedom, and no ability to see the universal concept in a singular happening: It's all reds, no Red, all instances of a color and no concept of the color itself, endless singular motions, no "going for a walk." They are unruled *and therefore unfree*.

This may seem odd, but for Kant, freedom means to give oneself laws, and for Kant, lawgiving requires a sovereign. From this political biology, Kant draws the following conclusions: Animals and humans are cast into a sea of disorganized sensations, and humans are able to organize these sensations into ideas, to rule over them, but animals cannot. Therefore, animals are a people without a ruler, a chaotic mass of events with no central government; humans have a government to rule over sensuality (our minds). Kant keeps the premodern division between higher and lower faculties.

Kant's work is more dogmatic than that of the so-called dogmatists, many of whom sought to recuperate the "lower" faculties.[43] Here, Buber is—as so often—closer to Montaigne and Leibniz than is usually suspected. His "Hebrew humanism" relies (like all humanisms) on a distinction between humans and other animals, but it is not as harsh a distinction as that of Descartes and Kant. This is evident all the way down to the level of concepts: For Kant, the animal encounters "*only* the singularity of objects"; for Buber, it is precisely the singularity of objects and encounters that needs to be protected from the crude mechanism of the conceptual subordination machine.[44] For Buber, the distinction between humans and nonhuman animals is simply that humans can articulate and complete the disjunction between themselves and everything else—they can place things at an *articulated* distance—which is a mixed blessing.⁴⁵

For all three (Montaigne, Kant, and Buber), the human conceptual framework—the grid that "hangs together in space and time"—cuts the human off from dialogue with nonhuman beings.⁴⁶ Kant considers this to be good: Animals are "driven by natural instinct," whereas the human is free because he follows "only those [rules] that he himself *makes*."⁴⁷ We make our own rules, which is our inborn distinction from nature. For Montaigne, separating ourselves from other animals is humanity's original sin or, rather, "original distemper" and "presumption." We assume that we are so far elevated over other animals that we know them completely, including their "inward motivations."⁴⁸ To cure this arrogance, Montaigne prescribes skepticism to help us reconnect with the creaturely singularities we would elevate ourselves over. This entails giving up the belief that animals are machines whose workings are transparent to us. As Montaigne famously writes, "When I play with my cat, how do I know that she is not passing time with me rather than I with her?"⁴⁹

But even if we adopt the skeptical humanism of Montaigne over the dogmatic humanism of Kant—and let us say Buber falls between them (though he is certainly closer to Montaigne)—*how* can we talk to this animal? Do our differences prevent us from engaging in dialogue? For Kant, the answer is a clear yes. For Montaigne, the answer is a naive and enthusiastic no.⁵⁰ For Buber, the answer is more complicated: Dialogue, yes; speech, no. Like Montaigne, he illustrates this with a cat.

3

DOMESTIC CATS
Anxiety and Singularity

> The students of Rabbi Elazar asked him: For what reason does a dog recognize its master, while a cat does not recognize its master?
>
> —*Horayot 13a*[1]

CATS ARE USELESS, AND THE HISTORY OF THEIR domestication reflects this. Cats moved in because they wanted to, and we kept them because we like them.[2] Domestication has changed cats, but they are still very much like their undomesticated cousins. The primary differences between the two are size and sociality. Domestic cats are smaller, more communicative, and more social, whereas *Felis silvestris lybica* are solitary; domestic cats, even when running wild, enjoy the existence of other cats.[3] Finally, the range and frequency of their sounds increase (such as the meows made when they want attention), and "apart from when they are in heat... and when they are angry, adult cats do not usually 'talk' to each other. The sounds they make are mostly for our human ears."[4] Cats communicate with us and for us. The same can be said of our conversations with them.

People who think in terms of species rather than individuals (like Haraway or Deleuze) seem to gravitate toward dogs, while philosophers concerned with singulars seem to prefer cats. As Soseki writes, "To the casual observer it may appear that all cats are the same, facsimiles in form and substance, as indistinguishable as peas in a pod; and that no cat can lay claim to individuality. But once admitted to feline society, that casual observer would very quickly realize that things are not so simple, and that the human saying that 'people are freaks' is equally true in the world of cats."[5]

From Montaigne onward, we find countless examples of cat vignettes in the work of those enamored by idiosyncrasy.[6] Modern Jewish thought presents a subtradition of these: Buber depicts a cat encounter in *I and Thou*, which is later transposed into the work of Hans Jonas, Rachel Adler, and Derrida.[7] Buber's cat encounter also sparked criticism: His friend Rosenzweig told him that Buber's affinity for cats demonstrated an unseriousness about relationships with God.[8] Hagiographers, biographers, detractors, and even the author of a children's book have noted Buber's affection for cats.[9]

Buber had nine (nine!) cats in Jerusalem, which were cared for by the Dajani family when the Bubers were forced to flee Abu Tor.[10] These cats would walk in and out of his windows, as described in Schalom Ben-Chorin's quaint anecdote: "There were cats in the room and Buber would speak to them. In the summer the window was open and the cats would jump in and out. Once a cat jumped in and Buber asked it, 'Where did you come from, I haven't seen you for quite a while.' I felt as if the cats understood what Buber said to them."[11] Buber would surely have appreciated this.

We begin with an interpretation of the famous cat encounter in *I and Thou* and end with Derrida's revision of the same scene. The encounter begins as follows:

> The eyes of an animal have the capacity of a great language [*Sprache*]. Independent, without any need of the assistance of sounds and gestures, most eloquent when they rest entirely in their glance, they express the mystery in its natural captivity, that is, in the anxiety of becoming. This state of the mystery is known only to the animal, which alone can open it up to us—for this state can only be opened up [*eröffnen*] and not revealed [*offenbaren*]. The language in which this is accomplished *is what it says*: anxiety [*Bangigkeit*—can also be translated as "nervousness"]—the stirring of the creature between the realms of plantlike security and spiritual risk. This language is the stammering of nature under the initial grasp of spirit, before language yields to spirit's cosmic risk which we call man. But no speech [*Reden*] will ever repeat what the stammer is able to communicate [*mitzuteilen*].[12]

Buber opens with the broad category of the animal (not the cat) and presents several important elements. He claims that an animal's eyes have the capacity for language without any movement or gesture; this is not "body language." In Peircean terms, this "language" is not of symbols, nor is it made up of the indexes commonly used by animals. It is, instead, iconic: It "*is what it says*"—the "signified" and "signifier" are one and the same.[13] However, despite insisting that movement is unimportant, Buber is concerned only with animal life—moving life—in particular, animals with eyes. It seems that the movements that constitute life remain in the background.

Buber is crudely abstract in terms of both category (the animal) and communication, and he focuses on only one thing these animals' eyes communicate. What is this thing? Anxiety, specifically the anxiety of becoming, meaning the perpetual flux of life. Human speech [*Reden*] provides an anchor, a sense of stability. As speaking humans, we have lost touch with this anxiety and are thus unable to perform it.

From these extremely general opening reflections Buber moves to a more particular case: looking into the eyes of a house cat. "I sometimes look into the eyes of a house cat. The domesticated animal has not by any means received the gift of the truly 'speaking' [*sprechenden*] glance from us, as a human conceit suggests sometimes; what it has from us is only the ability—purchased with the loss of its elementary naturalness [*Unbefangenheit*]—to turn this glance on us brutes. In this process, some mixture of surprise and question has come into it, into its dawn and even its rise—and this was surely wholly absent from the original glance, for all its anxiety."[14]

Buber addresses the cat's domesticity out of the gate, which is neither an asset nor a deficiency. The domestic cat has "lost" its "elementary naturalness" because a "natural" cat wouldn't care about humans. So, the only thing that is "lost" is that a domestic cat is in the unfortunate position of finding humans and their company interesting. Both you and your cat are cultivated to pay attention to each other, and this increases the chance of dialogue. The cat doesn't gain speech from domestication, and domestication is not the reason it is anxious. It "speaks" as it speaks, and it is anxious because it is an animal. The domestication consists only of bringing you both together.

The paragraph continues: "Undeniably, *this* cat began its glance by asking me with a glance that was ignited by the breath of my glance: 'Can it be that you mean me? Do you actually want that I should not merely do tricks for you? Do I concern you? Am I there for you? Am I there? What is that coming from you? What is that around me? What is it about me? What is that?!'"[15]

We are now focusing on "this" cat while describing something that's happened several times with other cats. Buber describes an extremely common interaction: a skittish cat. Not a cat worried about something else, but worried about you: Are you paying attention to me? This is a common experience for anyone used to feline company.

Petting a cat much like playing an instrument or using a tool, is groove-like, a rhythmic interaction neither fully conscious nor unconscious. Focus too much on the specifics, and your hand lands on the notes awkwardly or incorrectly—the cat jumps. Forget it's happening, and it falls apart; you pet the cat backward and are rewarded with claws. "Groove" and dialogue are hardly identical, but both involve a mixture of intention and spontaneity alongside a relation to other creatures that is difficult to capture.

This is perhaps because cats, despite their love of attention, are extremely anxious or picky about it. A cat's concern that you are "really there," its worry that you might not be being intentional about your engagement with it, as complex as it is common. This is why Buber presents a vignette and not an argument: If you have never had this interaction with a cat, you're not going to get it. Much like the thought experiment that opens this book, if you don't know what it means for a cat to signal "Can it be that you mean me?" it will be impossible to convince you of the actuality of this second-person question in my third-person language.

From "Am I there *for you*?" the vignette proceeds along the path to a darker question: "Am I there?"[16] If the "I" is always hyphenated, always in a *relation* (to a you or an it), the same applies to a cat, even if it doesn't have an "I" in a straightforward manner (because it doesn't use language).[17] When the other person leaves an encounter abruptly, we might experience dizzy confusion (like the confusion we feel exiting a dark theater in the middle of a sunny day). Buber imagines this moment, as even more intense for the cat than it is for us, because the cat lacks the support of language and so is entirely turned over to becoming.[18]

This vignette-encounter has steadily narrowed its focus, from the category of animal, to the house cat, to an individual cat. It's not a seamless transition, and the final move from types (animals, cats) to a specific being ("this cat") is not a question of degree but a shift from a group to a singularity. A singular being, by definition, is not part of a group, but is what happens when we think of something only as an individual. Because singulars aren't in a group we can't identify them by characteristics (because that puts them into a group). Instead, we use names, point, or use a pronoun. Buber uses pronouns to identify his cat. But his cat can't use a pronoun to identify him. Cats don't say *I* or *you* or anything else, so we must think differently about them than we do about ourselves.

Addressing this (necessary) distortion, Buber continues: "'I' is here a paraphrase [*Umschreibung*] of a word of I-less self-reference *that we lack*. 'That' represents the flood of man's glance in the entire actuality of its power to relate."[19]

Buber doesn't want to claim humans are superior in terms of dialogue but that there is a serious difference between the species concerning the pronoun *I*, a pronoun central to Buber's thinking. Here, a lot of work occurs very quickly and it's easy to miss. Humans "have" an "I" (we are always hanging around ourselves), but we are not identical with it. I am far vaster than the point-sized transcendental ego indicated by a pronoun or even the more robust ego theorized by Freud. This "I" exists only alongside another pronoun. So, you can have "I-It" or "I-You," but there is no I without IT or YOU (and the dash connecting them).[20] So far, so good, but what to do with animals who do not say "I" about themselves? This cannot be skipped over.[21]

The animal in dialogue does not say "I" or "you," even if they may indicate them. Buber suggests we use a placeholder here. It is an unsatisfying solution but it has the great merit of avoiding unnecessary anthropomorphism.[22] When we find ourselves in a dialogue with a cat, who has no "I," we paraphrase to indicate the "word of I-less self-reference *that we lack*." We know the cat has a sense of self, but we don't know how it works; we know cats can direct their attention to others, but because they cannot talk we don't know how that works either. It's not that cats lack a sense of self or other but rather that the cat and I relate to these completely differently.

Once you start using language you become inextricably tied to it, and it is nearly impossible to recollect what life was before the transformation. The "I" stabilizes the self, gives it a sense of being (rather than becoming). The cat's "self-reference"—as relational as our own—is also called a *word* [*Wort*], but its workings and basic intentional structures are left unexplained. I cannot help but wish Buber had used a different term, but it does have the merit of showing the language-like structures of self and intentionality.

The brief encounter with the cat finished, Buber moves from talking-to to talking-about, to figure out what we can *learn* from such encounters: "There the glance of the animal, the language of anxiety, had risen hugely—and set almost at once. . . . It is for the sake of the language of this barely perceptible rising and setting of the spirit sun that I relate this minute occurrence. . . . No other event has made me so deeply aware of the evanescent actuality *in all relationships to other beings*, the sublime melancholy [*erhabne Schwermut*] of our lot, the fated lapse into It of every single You."[23]

The animal—in this case, the cat—is the preeminent bearer of anxiety about becoming because the animal knows anxiety in a way we cannot. Much as speech irrevocably transforms our sense of self, it also eases our nervousness about becoming by hiding it from us. The cat "owns" anxiety because it knows and expresses it better than we can.

But the melancholy, which is structural, is shared. This melancholy—that all relationships end—was resented by many of Buber's followers almost as much as they resented his inclusion of the cat in a sphere they'd have marked "humans only." One consequence of the I-You's exclusivity is that it is transitory by nature: Not only will it end, but you should want it to, even if that makes you sad. The I-You ends not only because you have a poor attention span, but because if it doesn't end, *it becomes meaningless* because it won't affect anything. Buber's preoccupation with the "melancholy [*Schwermut*] of our lot" is thus not, as Kaufmann suggests, the psychological "generalization" of a romantic mind but rather a fundamental principle without which Buber's work doesn't make sense. The singular exclusive relation (and all I-You relations are singular and exclusive) is not itself a thing, so if you want the relationship to affect things (including other people), then it has to stop being singular and enter into the common world. Responding to the singular means we make it real. Realization in the world of things means the relation disappears so I can go about making actual changes.[24]

Cats probably don't care about these distinctions. But the cat bears anxiety and illustrates melancholy in part because the "speaking" is done not with words but with glances. To beat a dead horse, language, for all its virtues, can distract us from the situation of dialogue. Language may not be permanent but it is infinitely reproducible, and this creates the illusion of permanence. In this sense, language is indeed the "house of being," while a dialogue without language takes place closer to world of becoming.[25]

Everything I've discussed so far concerns an intense I-You encounter with a cat. The case of dialogue is thankfully not so extreme. It has periods of intensity and latency that mirror the "rising and setting of the spirit sun," but it is comfortable residing in the normal world for periods of time. Perhaps dialogue's chief distinction from the I-You is that dialogue lacks the all-or-nothing exclusivity of the absolute encounter. It has a different temporality and can survive waxing and waning. Buber's concept of love (which is a relationship, not a feeling) is thus closer to dialogue than it is to the I-You, "It is not the relationship that necessarily wanes, but the actuality of its directness. *Love itself cannot abide in a direct relation; it endures, but in the alternation of actuality and latency.* Every You in the world is compelled by its nature to become a thing for us or at least to enter again and again into thing-hood."

This relationship—more a commitment than a feeling—not only can but in fact *must* survive between moments of intense encounter. It is only in this back-and-forth that love is real, both a real thing and a real nonthing: intense encounter followed by the mundane drudgery of maintaining a relationship or a household.[26] If love cannot survive outside of pure encounters then it's merely an affair for beautiful souls.[27]

So, too, with a cat. You can pet a cat and move from moments where you are both and then scratch her head so she is comfortable and secure again. You can dialogue through the movement of your hand on her fur, and this can be intense or unthinking. Buber's cat in *I and Thou* is there to illustrate the moment of spontaneity and reciprocity, but as I listen to my son in the next room explaining to our cat at great length how amazing his fur is, I understand that this little encounter is neither a pure giving over to absolute otherness, nor is it merely my son's ego projecting itself onto a screen made of fur. It's a bit of column A, a bit of column B. Reciprocity, or mutuality (which is as close as Buber gets to defining *relation* in the broad sense), is not always so intense as absolute presence. Head-scratching works just as well sometimes.

Afterwords and Afterlives of Buber's Cats

For Levinas, the very fact that Buber is able to have an encounter with a cat demonstrates the poverty of his thought. His objection is not that "things" (all nonhuman beings) don't really reciprocate (as one might expect); rather, he doesn't approve of the reciprocation. That dialogue with animals is held to be *possible* disfigures Buber's thinking because it is obvious to Levinas that such relationships are neither ethical nor "vertical."[28] For Levinas, "Man . . . is a being sui generis," and reciprocity with animals violates this because it suggests that nonhumans and humans have more in common than Levinas would like.[29]

Thus, he writes, "the ethical aspects of the I-Thou relation, so frequently evoked in Buber's *descriptions* are not determinant, and the I-Thou relation is also possible with respect to things."[30] He is correct here on both counts:

Ethics does not determine relationships, and intimacy and reciprocity can be achieved with "things." Levinas senses this latter point and dislikes it: "Buber *admitted* that things too can enter into the I-Thou relation."[31] As if it were a crime.

Levinas is wrong because he is right. He is correct that Buber thinks dialogue with animals is possible, and he is correct that this means dialogue is not *fundamentally* ethical. If you want your fundamental relationship to be inexorably ethical then Buber is not the thinker for you. If cats and humans can dialogue, then dialogue is not a great criterion for ethical decisions—unless you think cats and humans are of equal ethical value, which I don't, Buber didn't, and most other people don't either.[32]

We find a more sympathetic reading in Jonas, who puts Buber's cat to work for the sake of his philosophy.[33] For Jonas, animal dialogue provides a path between universality (human nature is uniform) and relativity (people are radically different). Our shared animality provides a familiarity that keeps us on the same page when we interpret events: "The basis of this familiarity is the community of animal nature, and in the case of intra-specific relations, the community of the species. A creature recognizes greed or aggression when it meets it in a fellow creature's eyes . . . and this far beyond its own kind."[34] Animal community becomes the basis for a shared phenomenology that reaches beyond the human species. Jonas's entire project depends not on biological proximity—or even sharing life—but on the fact that we can *communicate* across species.

At issue is dialogue, and thus a reciprocity on which we can build more complex forms of "understanding and misunderstanding":

> The cat looks up at my eyes, *she seeks my glance*, she wants something from me. Nobody has taught her that these are the body parts with which I notice her, and in which my noticing or not-noticing becomes visible to her. She "knows": she can reach me that way. And I, too, do not need information from physiology and neurology in order to feel here a gaze on me and to read the entreaty in it; intuitive physiognomies is at work. We look at each other, and something passes between us without which there could be no higher understanding, however far it surpasses this elemental stratum.[35]

This remix of Buber's cat encounter serves to illustrate a "natural groundwork" for shared language and truth. Like Buber, Jonas draws philosophical implications from this meeting: It illuminates key elements of Jonas's "system." Where Buber's cat teaches us about dialogue without language,

Jonas uses a cat to argue that human language is only possible *because* we can have wordless communication underneath it. Our "shared organic basis" serves as a "natural groundwork" for "invented, constructed, and freely manipulated expressions and symbols," not because of proximity between our genomes or analogy based on our "inner life" but because animals can talk-to one another.[36]

When Jonas writes, "The cat looks up at my eyes, she seeks my glance," his cat is not watching him and then inferring some hidden mental state; his cat sees his gaze. It is reading him, not his signals.[37] Here, too, the negative—essential for any hermeneutics—enters, if inchoately: "Nobody has taught her that these are the body parts with which I notice her, and in which my noticing or not-noticing becomes visible to her." Buber's cat's anxiety ("Do you really mean me?") is given a different but compatible explanation: The cat can see you not-seeing and is as attuned to this as it is to your seeing.

Before moving on to Derrida, it's worth mentioning that Buber received enough interrogations about animals and "nature" in *I and Thou* that he devoted the first part of his 1957 afterword to these topics. That this was a prominent concern among early readers seems to have been forgotten by the slew of Buber interpreters who seek to preserve him as a good Jew rather than a good thinker. He begins his afterword by noting that he's often asked about the difference between a human I-You and a nonhuman one, and how any reciprocity is possible with nonhumans. His response to this opens a line of thinking that Derrida inherits: If we want to talk about an encounter with nonhumans, the first thing we need to do is abandon the uniform notion of nature.

So, "nature" as a monolith that opposes human beings is a flawed concept. It needs to be divided up into *Bezirke*: "realms," "fields," or, better, "districts."[38] But how to divide these? This taxonomy is not going to be biological. As noted, Buber's early work uses the standard pseudo-Aristotelian taxonomy: plants, animals, humans. His later work is no more scientific than this (nor need it be), but it has been modified to account for the different dialogical possibilities that species possess. Hence, what he adds to the usual Aristotle-Germanic division is domestication:

> Man once "tamed" animals, and he is still capable of bringing off this strange feat. *He draws animals* into his own sphere [*Atmosphäre!*] and moves them to accept him, a stranger, in an elementary manner and to accede to his ways. He *obtains from them an often astonishing active response* to his approach, to

his address—and on the whole this response is the stronger and more direct, the more his relation amounts to a genuine You-saying.... outside the tamed circle [*Zähmungsbezirks*], too, we occasionally encounter a similar contact between men and animals: some men have deep down in their being a potential partnership with animals.[39]

Animals who live in our *Atmosphäre* are given pride of place. The word *tamed* is placed in scare quotes, and once more, domestication means little more than "now they put up with us and sometimes even listen to us."

Atmosphäre-animals are the only ones in Buber's animal dialogues. A Viennese dandy, he did not try to commune with bears. The distinction between domestic and wild shifts depending on the people involved, but that doesn't mean it isn't there or that it shouldn't be respected. Timothy Treadwell, the subject of the documentary film *Grizzly Man*, developed dialogical relationships with bears, but this did not prevent him from being slaughtered by one. The domestic/wild distinction is permeable: We occasionally dialogue with animals outside the home; there are exceptional people who do so routinely. But domestication is the very first distinction Buber draws within "nature" because the distinction is dialogical, not biological.[40]

Derrida's Cat

Who told you that you were naked?

—God

Derrida's *The Animal That Therefore I Am* weaves together multiple texts with a vignette. This scene which holds the texts together is borrowed from Buber (who is barely mentioned).[41] This is typical of Derrida who rarely cites Buber, but when he does it is approvingly and as a foil for a criticism of Levinas.[42] Derrida rarely dwells on things he actually likes.[43]

Like Buber's, the scene is a cat encounter, but with three important shifts: The anxiety is Derrida's (not the feline's), the encounter takes place in Derrida's house, and Derrida is naked. While Derrida infamously never leaves the textual, an encounter—a "real" encounter—holds the readings together: "I must immediately make it clear, the cat I am talking about is a real cat, truly, believe me, a little cat."[44] Encounters with animals who don't speak highlight one of philosophy's limitations: its absolute dependence on language, even in its visual-phenomenological variations.[45] It is thus not insignificant that when Derrida tries his hand at the animal problem textuality is brought to circle around a "real" encounter.

Derrida brings an odd amount of sophistication to the problem of Buber's cat. He lacks Buber's naiveté about encounter and is attentive to the fact that real encounters require (at minimum) textuality to be conveyed. Nonlanguage requires language, which is here not a paradox so much as a problem. When Derrida calls the cat "real," making clear this is not a reading or a poem but a bathroom encounter, he unsurprisingly (but gleefully) does so with a citation from a book: the word *real* comes from another famous cat encounter, Lewis Carroll's *Through the Looking Glass*, which begins with Alice falling asleep while talking to a cat and ends with her return to reality. The return to reality occurs in chapter 11, reproduced here in full:

> CHAPTER XI
> Waking
> —and it really *was* a kitten, after all.

The dream/reality division is never "solved" in Carroll's books; if nothing else, logic operates across the divide—it is as weird in the waking world as it is in the sleeping world. Derrida continues this weirdness, using a citation from a book to insist that he is not talking about a book.

Buber constantly speaks about what cannot be spoken *about*. But where Buber falls back on pointing, trying to break out of the circle with indexes, stories, and tricks (like Kierkegaard), Derrida tries to exhaust the system itself, bringing it to the point where its contradictions are seen but not surpassed (like Kierkegaard).

While he clearly approves of Buber's attempts to indicate the supralogical, Derrida is not optimistic about our ability to do so without reverting to a jargon of authenticity or obscuring the violence hidden in our metaphysical heritage. Thus, where Buber points and invokes, Derrida circles and deflates. Both approaches (as with all philosophical habits) can be annoying, but Derrida's "real" cat interrupts this circling long enough for him to craft what is perhaps his most effortless talk.

Derrida avoids Buber's crude rendering of nature and the thick, heavy lines he uses to outline the figures within it. He does not, however, simply replace them with blurred lines, liminal spaces, spectrums, or any other such half-measures. Instead, he forces us to come to terms with the paradoxes that singularity causes, and he uses these to variegate nature.

Derrida repeats Buber's cat encounter in a biblical-mundane key: Naked and ashamed in front of his cat, Derrida wonders whether clothing might not be a better human/animal distinction than the usual one (language). The human, the animal that clothes itself, is perhaps the only animal that can be naked. Nietzsche claims that we flatter ourselves with clothing; we say we dress to cover up our animal parts, but in reality, we clothe ourselves to cover up how unanimal, how flimsy and effete we are.[46] The lack of clothing is a lack felt only by humans.

But why feel shame in front of a cat? Perhaps because Derrida encounters his cat in the bathroom, and this room is as shameful for him as the Talmud claims the litterbox is for cats?.[47] Derrida quite consciously has put his cat in the position of God, and the bathroom becomes the Garden of Eden, where God, in a terrifying display of ignorance, indignantly asks Adam, "Who told you that you were naked?" God, presumably naked himself, asks the most Freudian question in the Hebrew Bible.[48] The answer is, of course, that no one has told him. Evading responsibility, Adam blames Eve, who in turn blames the serpent.

There is a secret path between Cat and God that is duplicated in Buber's three spheres. The first and the third sphere (life with nature and life with spiritual beings) are both marked by their distance from normal human language. And both God and Cat are unnamed. Buber's "cat" is also unnamed, but it isn't "one" cat; he is relating an experience that he has had "several times." Derrida, more a monotheist, refers to a single instance and a single cat. The situation is singular, even if the language is citational (and therefore shared).

Those who see naming as a sort of violence have made much of the fact that Derrida doesn't tell us the cat's name.[49] The violence of naming is lost on me. What interests me is that names are one of the two standard ways to indicate singulars (pronouns are the other) and Derrida is trying to refer to a singular being without using either of them. But Derrida is not "unnaming"—the cat has a name; he just doesn't tell us what it is.

After insisting he is not going to perform a "negative zootheology," Derrida nonetheless proceeds by negation—telling us what his cat is "not." An unsurprising consequence of wanting to position the encounter within an intellectual genealogy, Derrida presents and dissects a small history of cat theology by telling us who his cat isn't. This cat is supposedly an allegory, nor is it part of Kafka's "zoopoetics," or Hoffman's, or Montaigne's.[50] And then we find this: "Nor does the cat that looks at me naked, she and no other, the one

I am talking about here, belong, although we are getting warmer, to Baudelaire's family of cats, or Rilke's, or Buber's. *Literally, at least, these poets' and philosophers' cats don't speak.*"[51] Derrida will, of course, play with the notion of speaking, but his cat, being a cat, also doesn't.

How is Derrida's cat different from Rilke's or Buber's? To note two differences, his cat is gendered and it is not an "ambassador." She "does not appear here to represent, like an *ambassador, the immense symbolic responsibility with which our culture has always charged the feline race.*"[52] Instead, she is a "real cat," a creature of "unsubstitutable singularity," meaning she is this and nothing else, and nothing can take her place, whereas Buber's cat encounter has happened several times. Buber begins within the general, even as he speaks about a (repeatable) singularity.

The relationship between dialogue and repetition now gets another wrinkle. As mentioned, Buber and his cat, in giving up the repeatability of language, reveal the delicate and flimsy ground of dialogue. But we now see that a type of repetition remains, one revealed when we treat *Felis catus* as a species. If I want to talk about "cat dialogues" as a category, then I am using general concepts, speaking about "cats." Generalization is necessary if we want to think about types of nonhuman dialogues, but it is a problem, a conflict between talking-to and talking-about, between dialogue and analysis. Derrida develops the problem: Even if we don't talk-about dialogue, dividing dialogues up into different types (or species) invokes generalizations that conflict with the singularity of the encounter. So how should we talk about these singularities?

Derrida claims there are "only two types of discourse" regarding the animal.[53] While plainly false, his distinction is useful: On one side, we have the philosophers (from Descartes to Levinas), and on the other, "poets or prophets."[54] According to Derrida, the philosophers all share a basic position, which is that the animal has no language or is "deprived" of language.[55] It is easy to be confused; surely, the "poets" don't think animals can speak English.

To understand what he means let's look at Rilke's "Black Cat," which presents an eye-to-eye encounter where we see the cat seeing and it in turn sees us seeing. Rilke's cat speaks the language of the eyes with more authority than Buber's does; with Rilke's cat, "your strongest gaze will be absorbed and utterly disappear":

She seems to hide all looks that have ever fallen
into her, so that, like an audience,
she can look them over, menacing and sullen,

>   and curl to sleep with them. But all at once
>   as if awakened, she turns her face to yours;
>   and with a shock, you see yourself, tiny,
>   inside the golden amber of her eyeballs
>   suspended, like a prehistoric fly.[56]

If the greatest danger for animal dialogue is projection, Rilke provides a guardrail against it.[57] Our potential projection is acknowledged and blocked by the cat; the cat's eye contains you as an object in two senses. The cat sees you, but she also sees you seeing her. If projection is what happens when we play both parts in the dialogue (and the cat is merely a screen), here, the opposite occurs: The cat sees us projecting onto it, and this becomes the cat's object.

Are we constitutive for Rilke's cat? It's impossible to know, but the cat has flipped from being seen, to seeing us see it, to seeing our seeing. It may begin on the stage (the object, the screen), but she is hardly a celebrity. She isn't even watching us (looking for approval); she is watching us watch, and that is her object. She's the audience: "And with a shock, you see yourself, tiny."

Here, as with many poetic fancies, we are given neither evidence nor argument, just a shape. In this case it is the shape of an encounter with the cat where we are not "dethroned" (as many would have The Animal do for us) but treated as an object of gentle condescension. Is this a dialogue? No, because the cat has not engaged, but the ability to disengage is a necessary condition for certain types of dialogue.[58]

So, what really distinguishes poets from philosophers is not what they think about language but—much as with Buber—the language-like: the language of the eyes, or the gaze. It is easier to understand this visually. The philosophers look at the animal, but they don't see the animal looking at them. "Their gaze has never intersected with that of an animal directed at them." The poets, however, see themselves being seen. We can say that the philosopher talks-about the animal, but the poet talks-with the animal because she sees the animal looking at her.[59]

For Derrida's poet, animals can respond to you (and vice versa), whereas his philosopher does not feel *addressed* by the animal: "Even those who, from Descartes to Lacan, have conceded to the animal some aptitude for signs and for communication have always denied it the power to *respond*."[60] Among the philosophers, there is no reciprocation between the animal and the human being. There is, in short, no dialogue and no responsibility.

Without address and response, there is, for Derrida, no space for ethical operations like shame; his own shame is a response to being addressed by the cat. Presumably, the cat has no interest in shaming him (at least, not for his nakedness). Uncharitably, this is a form of projection or confusion on Derrida's part. But, arguably, that's not what's happening here. Derrida's point is that once you open yourself up to a dialogue, or think of the animal as capable of response, otherwise absent ethical and emotional forces come into play. So, yes, it's a projection, but it's the sort of projection that occurs in all dialogue. That this is an indirect citation of Genesis 3:11 is on point: Adam and God dialogue, even if their interaction is beset with confusion and judgment.

If philosophers have no dialogue, no exchange of glances, what do we get from the so-called poets and prophets? Derrida's poet, ironically, aligns fairly closely with Heidegger's work, despite Heidegger being ranked among the philosophers. The poet doesn't *use* animals (or anything) but instead just lets them be what they are and then conceals this being from us. But the way the poet re-conceals is also revealing.[61] So far, so good. Our problem is that Derrida assumes (falsely) that this poetic or prophetic relationship exists in sharp contrast to the everyday. But are there not everyday and domestic activities that also accomplish this letting be? Can one not loaf around the house? Derrida encounters his cat in the bathroom, after all.

According to Derrida, we have made a fundamental mistake when we think about language. We assume that language is primarily spoken and that writing is a weird derivative of speech.[62] Obviously, this is historically true—speech appears first—but history can trick us into thinking the *essence* of language is speech, and writing is just an echo of this talking. What does this mean? I say a sentence: "That kid looks tired." The meaning of this sentence can be detached from my speech, from the way I say it. Perhaps you repeat, "That kid looks tired." Your voice (and therefore your speech) *sounds* entirely different from mine, but the content remains the same. Now have a friend repeat it in sign language. All sound has disappeared into their hand movements. Write it down; it's now blue and white symbols. Type it on a computer, and a batch of 1s and 0s maintains it.

This is what I mean when I say that language creates artificial stability—not that the words live on eternally, humming away in God's mind, but that the *content* of dialogue is recordable, repeatable.[63] In this sense, Derrida's confusing claims about the primacy of writing can be made useful:

Symbol systems precede speech logically (but not historically). From this point, Derrida launches his many-fronted war on artificial stability, such as his critique of metaphysics which takes aim at the patriarchal home and patriarchal metaphysics (phallogocentrism).

The problem is that this critique of stability in turn rests on a critique of the "everyday" which obscures as much as it reveals: "'Everyday language' is not innocent or neutral. It is the language of Western metaphysics, and it carries with it not only a considerable number of presuppositions of all types but also presuppositions inseparable from metaphysics, which, although little attended to, are knotted into a system."[64]

How is everyday language the language of metaphysics, when metaphysical prose is recondite and tortured? Derrida is claiming that I think the same way when doing metaphysics as I do when I am working (rather than what I do when I read poetry). One response is to say that metaphysics is based in geometry, not language, and so Derrida is wrong. But you still need to give reasons for *why* I should base metaphysics on geometry, and these reasons are made in everyday language. The same goes for any technical language: I need to give *reasons* for adopting a technical language, and these reasons are made in everyday language. I am not allowed to justify the use of a technical language with poetry or ecstasy; at some point, I need to use "normal" arguments, and here, the language of the everyday comes into play.

This is a development of Nietzsche's argument that grammar and everyday language determine our thinking.[65] Hence, Derrida's claim that everyday language secretly forms and affirms theological, social, and political positions. This seems correct. He errs by supposing that the only antidote is poetic language.[66] Indeed, reading *The Animal*, one gets the impression that those with a tin ear for poetry are doomed to shoddy metaphysics because they are mired in everyday language. But this is not the case. Derrida and Heidegger *are* correct that everyday reasoning (and not, say, poetic reasoning) is the basis of metaphysics. They err in having a limited notion of the everyday. For them, the language of the everyday is uncritical, masculine business language, and they are rightfully afraid that this language, with its emphasis on "identifying problems," "finding solutions," and "understanding the situation," will generate an uncritical and derivative metaphysics that merely repeats crystalized prejudice in a more refined key.[67]

But must we become amateur poets to challenge this? I suggest we can look at the everyday with greater care and find other paths there. If metaphysics is based in "everyday language" (which it is), then should we not ask, *Which* everyday language? What are the other languages of the everyday? There are several, and I propose gossip and other forms of domestic reasoning as an alternative to business-speak. Critique is found in gossip and the hallway, and by attending to this, a more critical form of thought is possible.[68]

The Thin Furry Line

Derrida rejoins our project when he (rather prosaically) tries to distinguish animals from humans. His distinctions are drawn to retain generic differences (the differences between "human" and "cat") while still allowing for singular encounters across them He also deviates from fashionable materialisms by rejecting attempts to annul the differences between humans and animals: "There is no interest to be found in debating something like a discontinuity, rupture, or even abyss between those who call themselves men and what so-called men, those who name themselves men, call the animal. Everybody agrees on this. . . . *Even animals know that.*"[69] This is a welcome antidote to the far too common position that identifying our differences is something we impose on animals. Derrida's cat is completely aware it is not human. Awareness of the difference from human beings is common across all household animals.

Where things get interesting is *how* Derrida views this border. It is not (as with Simondon and Agamben) drawn within the human, nor is it drawn externally as is done by common sense; it is drawn between *and* within, by both him *and his cat*. However, as Derrida leaves his bathroom encounter and focuses on the theory things get so messy that he is forced to advance multiple versions of the same thesis: that the line is a problem. The line distinguishing him from his cat is a mess but still conceivable within the encounter (by him and the cat); however, the line distinguishing humans from other animals is a mess of messes.

Derrida thus proceeds from the singular to the particular to the general, producing three versions of his thesis that we can simplify as follows: The line is an "abyssal rupture," and so it doesn't have just two edges (the human on one side and the animal on the other); this "border" has a history;

and, finally, there is no Animal, just lots of different animals, each requiring its own line.[70] In sum, there is no line between humans and animals because there are multiple *types* of lines (self-divided, separating, connecting, drawn through, drawn by one, drawn by both, etc.) and there is no Animal just lots of different types of animals. The line between a cat and I is not the same as a line drawn between me and a gecko.

Derrida opposes his way of distinguishing between humans and other animals to the way other philosophers do it: "All philosophers have judged that limit to be single and indivisible, considering that on the other side of that limit there is an immense group, a single and fundamentally homogeneous set."[71] But what does Derrida's prophet or poet get us, other than a proliferation of differences? Is this just adding "nuance"?[72] If so, Derrida is of no value; he does little more than gesture that "it's complicated." Do I really need his cat to help me with that? But what of the *way* the line is drawn? Derrida's value lies in recognizing that the *way* the line is drawn, and even the type of line, has to do with the animal's specific differences from us. Thus we need to think about species, about types, about general characteristics, in our animal dialogues. Perhaps the I-You can ignore this difference and luxuriate in the meeting of two singularities, but dialogue has to account for the differences and particular traits of partners.

Derrida's cat is thus not merely "theoretically" helpful but also an example of how dialogues, actual dialogues, can help us rethink and redraw the lines between us and animals. Where Buber's cats teach us about the anxiety of an encounter unanchored by language, Derrida's cat (singular) shows us a way to move from the singular to the individual, from a singular organism to a member of a type, not by "allowing" the cat to draw a line, but by seeing the line as the cat is drawing it.

How far can we generalize here? Not far. Moving from the singular to the universal is not going to work. Derrida's cat teaches you about itself, perhaps about other cats, perhaps about yourself, but not much more. This "experience" of a line drawn also by the animal, where the line does not merely separate and connect but runs right through you, is a household affair, hence its lack of violence. This is not a line on a map but a case of overlapping worlds. I breathe in my cat's dander and stray hairs, it licks the sweat from my hands, and we fight over space on the bed and for my children's affection.

It is this line that divides itself—otherwise known as a shared world—that leads writers to pen saturated and chaotic paragraphs when trying to describe animal encounters. Derrida's value is to maintain the line and the creatures on either side of it; on our side, citations, a language formed of words we inherit; on the other, a judgmental cat. The line is drawn not above by a third party, nor (as too many theory partisans assume) entirely by us and our language. The line is instead part of the meeting: It is there before the dialogue, it is occupied or divided during it, it shifts between encounters, and it remains there when it is over to inform the next encounter with this cat or another. How do dialogues become "real"? Buber is frustratingly vague here, but Derrida provides something concrete: Animal dialogues, including judgmental ones, expose and shift the lines between us and other creatures.

Zooming Out

How do you dialogue with a cat? By talking to it, petting it, and—for the two writers' cats discussed here—looking at it looking at you. Dialogue is a common relationship with uncommon (singular) beings. The move between the general categories of the relation and the singularity of the creatures involved (between cats in general and a specific cat) requires us to mobilize tools and methods both within and outside of dialogue. This book stands outside of dialogue, the moving of a boundary by Derrida's cat, within it.

What we cannot do is pretend these lines have been canceled or that all our conversation partners are the same. Groups and lines, kinds and types, these cannot be overcome by fiat, and if we try to do so, we end up being unjust to the beings we encounter.[73] It would be not only cruel to expect the same kind of dialogue from a baby as from an adult or from a cat as a dog; it would also be stupid.

4

PLANTS
Dispersion and Surfaces

> I am a lover of knowledge, and the men who dwell in the city
> are my teachers, and not the trees or the country.
>
> —Socrates[1]

ANIMALS, ESPECIALLY MAMMALS, ARE PROBABLY THE EASIEST NONHUMANS to dialogue with. There are various reasons for this—many animals are social, emit sounds, and use sign systems—but movement is central. Animals move in roughly the same way and at the same tempo as humans do; both the tortoise and the hare possess locomotion and gestures on which we can base a folk psychology.[2] With animals, Buber's belief in nonhuman encounters is easily accepted. This is not the case for things that don't move or, like plants, that move very differently than we do. The slow movement of plant life can, however, help attune us to the time of dialogue. Where the I-You encounter is fast and takes only an instant—or, at most, a moment—dialogue can be stretched out over days or years, a fact easily missed when we restrict ourselves to human communication. Once more, it is the difficulties of plant dialogues that make them useful for theory.

That said, it's easy to sympathize with Hugo Bergman, who writes to Buber: "In preparing for my lecture I went through your *I and Thou* once more, and I noticed two difficulties which I did not mention in my lecture but do want to mention to you. One is the mutuality of the I-Thou relationship when the partner is an animal, a plant, or a stone. In my lecture, I emphasized that you did not mean empathy, which is a one-sided relationship, but true mutuality. I must confess, however, that things are not quite clear to me when the dialogue involves an inanimate partner."[3]

Bergman notes two concerns shared by many Buber interpreters: the need for mutuality and the fact that we verify mutuality by movement. It's easier to see mutuality with a cat than a stone because the cat shows its irritation by pulling back or scratching. But any mutuality with a plant will be experienced differently, or nonmutually, by the plant and I. What mutuality is for the plant and what it is for me are likely completely different. With most mammals, we can use movements to ensure we are on the same page. With a seemingly motionless plant, we are given no such security.

There is motionlessness and there is motionlessness, and, of course, from a certain angle, there is no motionlessness at all: At some scale and perspective anything can be put in motion. But with dialogue the only motion that matters communicates or creates intimacy. Plants do move. They gravitate toward light, know up from down, stretch roots, touch and coil around other plants, and shut down on insects to be devoured.[4] They move, but not at our pace. Here, tempo is a serious issue: Speed up a video of a plant and it looks conscious, but this isn't helpful when we're trying to dialogue.[5] Plants occupy a middle point between the seemingly motionless rock and the locomotive animal.

That said, the young Buber, drawing on Hasidic and Romantic sources, seemed to find dialogue with trees and plants relatively easy to comprehend. But as he aged, the philosophical problems with plant dialogue became more conspicuous. After noting the relative ease with which animal dialogue is possible, he wrote in 1957:

> It is altogether different with those realms of nature which lack the spontaneity that we share with animals. It is part *of our concept* of the plant that it cannot react to our actions upon it, that it cannot "reply." Yet this does not mean that we meet with no reciprocity at all here. We find here not the deed of posture of an individual being but a reciprocity of being itself [*Seins selber*]—a reciprocity that has nothing except being. The living wholeness and unity of a tree that denies itself to the eye, no matter how keen, of anyone who merely investigates, while it is manifest to those who say You, is present when they are present.... This huge sphere that reaches from the stones to the stars I should like to designate as the pre-threshold, meaning the step that comes before the threshold.[6]

I find this formulation extremely unsatisfying because "nothing except being" strikes me as both vague and evasive.[7] While Buber's solution is unappealing, his statement of the problem is good "Nature" is hardly homogeneous, and we must distinguish animal life from plants and other beings. And yes, the issue with plants is reciprocity: How do you know you're not merely projecting onto them? Dialogue is better able to deal with plant reciprocity than the I-You because dialogue is not as immediate as the encounter. The I-You occurs all at once and so is too fast for a plant; dialogue can be carried out over long periods of time, at a slower tempo, giving plants a chance to respond in a manner legible to us. Gardening can be understood as a form of dialogue with plant life—if you do something to annoy your plants, they will show you, in time, but not within the tight frame of a single encounter.

Greek Nature

Like many German Jews, Buber's model of nature was "Greek"; specifically, a standard reworking of Aristotle's kingdoms.[8] The model is not, however, concerned with precision: Buber's distinction between plants and animals has no explicit criterion.[9] The same is true for his distinction between living and nonliving beings. Phenomenologically speaking, the primary division is that animals have locomotion, and plants don't. The plant moves (grows, expands, bends, etc.), but it does so too slowly for most of us to engage immediately and spontaneously. And it does not travel. To plant something in the earth means to place it there.[10] This inability to travel (with some limited exceptions) is why, in classical Greek thought, plants were considered passive: "This kind of soul knows nothing of belief, reasoning, and intelligence, but is aware only of the pleasures and pains that accompany its appetites. Passivity is its constant and only mode of existence; it was not created with the gift of a natural capacity for self-consciousness or for rational thought about any aspect of itself (which are properties only of that which spins within itself and around its own centre, repelling external impulses while drawing on its own power of movement)."[11]

Ignoring the technical inaccuracies, Plato's philosophical mistake is to view plant life as passive on *our* terms. Plants do act to defend themselves, expel some things, and seduce others, among other easily missed movements.[12]

But Plato is hard to argue with on the question of interiority. Plants, in a word, don't have brains. They operate in a diffuse manner, different systems triggering each other without any central organization: They are dispersed. A clipping can be immersed in water and grow roots; roots can be severed from their body and produce more roots. Our self, or life, is centered in the head. While the power of the brain can be overstated, this is an insurmountable difference. Plants have no center, no "self," no "I," not even the

"I-like" status of a cat or a dog. They meet very few of the standard criteria for consciousness.[13]

This lack of interiority is a problem for dialogue in a way that a plant's supposed passivity is not. Despite many popular books arguing that trees talk, and the fact of chemical communication, any suggestion that plants use "language" requires stretching the concept to breaking point. It is worth asking: What is gained by this contortion? Arguably, the attempt to flatter plants by pretending we share characteristics debases them by assuming our characteristics are the only important ones. Plants are different.

So how do we dialogue with a being that has no interiority? Surely we can say You to them, but even this is complicated because a plant's limits are unclear. As Bergson notes, "It is hard to decide, even in the organized world, what is individual and what is not. The difficulty is great, even in the animal kingdom; with plants it is almost insurmountable."[14] To say You implies that the being we are directed toward is in some sense a "whole," or singular being. But massive plant systems complicate things: Where is a sumac tree? Is it the tree in front of you? Or is it the clonal colony it is a part of? Plants can expand our understanding of dialogue precisely because they can train us to direct ourselves toward a creature that is not bounded in the same way most people and things are. Arguably, I cannot say You to a mycelium network that occupies an uncertain number of hectares in the same way I say You to an object with clearer boundaries or a centralized interior.

In Freudian terms, the plant has no ego. In Peircean terms, while humans may use symbols, and other animals indexes, plants are largely iconic. There is a one-to-one relationship between any "sign" and its referent.[15] In phenomenological terms, plants are not intentional (there is no "as structure," etc.). No "as structure" means we do not appear to the plant as individuals. Chamovitz puts it bluntly: "An 'aware plant' is *not* aware of us as individuals."[16] Instead, the plant is dispersed and superficial. When we are enfolded in a forest, whether we dialogue with a single tree or the forest as a whole or the roots under the ground, the plant senses us only on its surfaces. To it, we are not an individual or singularity: "A plant is aware of its environment, and people are part of this environment. But it's not aware of the myriad gardeners and plant biologists who develop what they consider to be personal relationships with their plants. While these relationships may be meaningful to the caretaker, they are not dissimilar to the relationship between a child and her imaginary friend; the flow of *meaning* is unidirectional."[17]

This lack of meaning is important because the standard understanding of dialogue (one we are about to dispatch) is that dialogue is about meaning and its transmission.

But dialogue in Buber's sense orbits around encounters. And there is no reason to think we cannot encounter a plant. Marder provides a potential model: "'Plant-thinking' is in the first place the promise and the name of an encounter, and therefore it may be read as an invitation to abandon the familiar terrain of human and humanist thought and to meet vegetal life, if not in the place where it is, then at least *halfway*."[18] This is a dialogue where one participant (the plant) is a dispersed creature, a creature of surfaces. This doesn't mean it's more "available." If anything, surfaces are harder to dialogue with, and conceal more, than depths do. It *does* mean that plant encounters will be hampered by any stubborn anthropomorphism that insists on thinking of beings as individuals with clear outlines or as centrally organized systems of life. The vegetable's dispersion thus means any dialogue with it will have to dispense with naive anthropomorphism or crude anthropocentrism.

Again, we don't need to eliminate all traces of anthropocentrism. This book was written by a human, for humans, and it is concerned first and foremost with human beings. But human being is not self-sufficient. If we can learn anything from Buber (and those thinkers called "existential" or "phenomenological" or "Hegelian"), it's that part of what makes humans human is that we are constituted by otherness. For many (such as Levinas), this otherness is restricted to other-humans (with God a superhuman exception). Buber, despite his commitment to humanism, does not take this path.

Humans also exist in relation to nonhumans, and the nonhuman forms us too. Human being, in this sense, is nonhuman from the start. Avoiding crass anthropocentrism requires us to think about our nonhuman relationships. Plants are better than animals for this exercise. Animals are humanlike enough that an animal relationship can be viewed as merely a cruder form of human relationship (as with those who call their pets "fur babies"), but plants are too weird for this illusion to hold. Talking to mushrooms and trees can help us develop a qualified anthropocentrism. An anthropocentrism without superiority, one that is honest about our centrality to *ourselves*—and in the Anthropocene, a great deal of earthly life—without thinking we are the center of being or the universe or anything else.

Reading Buber and talking to trees won't rescue the planet, but our *presumed* inability to have dialogical relationships with nonhumans feeds an ecologically destructive crude anthropocentrism. Opening a dialogue with a plant will not stop a rapacious mining operation, but any model of thought that doesn't consider our intimate and spontaneous relationships with nonhumans is a poor thing.

Silencio

Plants are quiet and don't hear us—they are effectively silent. As a consummate talker I am no fan of quiet, but I will leave my predilection for chatter aside to explore what Buber could possibly mean when he claims dialogue or encounter can occur in silence.[19] There is no literal silence in the day-to-day. Listen carefully, and you will always hear something: the ambient noise amplified by a seashell, your own breathing, or, in my case, two children on the verge of conflict. Silence, like motionlessness, is a matter of perspective. What we mean by silence is a notable absence of sound, the lack of speech, or a volume low enough that we can go to sleep. For dialogue, silence means nothing more than not talking or making communicative noises.

There is a difference between our silence and the silence of plants. For us, it is a choice; for them, a condition. You cannot silence plants in the way I silence my son when I beg him to stop banging on the wall. Our silence can be seen as hiding or holding back, whereas a plant's silence is a simple fact. Any communication between plants is done wordlessly, and they do not miss language or feel its absence.

Silence does a lot of work for Buber. When he writes, "Only silence toward the You, the silence of all tongues, the taciturn waiting in the unformed, undifferentiated, prelinguistic word leaves the You free and stands together with it," he means that the only way to be with another creature without changing them or demanding anything of them, is to be "silent."[20] "All tongues" here presumably includes motion and sound. Silently being-with is a state some enter more easily with plants, and is a reason why, for them, gardens and trees are a refuge.[21] Dialogue, however, is closer to language than what occurs in this particular type of absolute silence. When Buber, in a different context, writes, "The *demanding* silence of forms, the loving speech of human beings, the *eloquent* muteness of creatures—all of these are gateways into the presence of the word," we are closer to the mark: Some silences demand things of us.[22]

Near the opening of *Dialogue*, Buber presents an example of "Das mitteilende Schweigen," or communicating silence.[23] Silence that communicates is exemplified here by two men sitting silently on a train, one calm, the other reserved. "Unreservedly communication [*Mitteilung*] streams from him, and the silence bears it to his neighbour.... He will be able to tell no one, not even himself, what he has experienced. What does he now 'know' of the other? No more knowing is needed. For where unreserve has ruled, even wordlessly, between men, the word of dialogue has happened sacramentally."[24]

Our task is to take this silence between two formed subjects on a train and transpose it into the home where the beings are more disparate. we also need to be more careful than Buber and avoid bombast about sacralization. The goal is not to make the garden a holy place—even if it might be for some people—but to tread carefully as we talk-about talking-to plants. As Irigaray asks, "How can we speak of the vegetal world? Is not one of its teachings to show without saying, or to say without words?"[25]

Levinas serves as an excellent guide. For him, the symptom, or evidence, that Buber's notion of relation is overly formal is what I suggest is its strength: that we can have relationships of responsibility—meaning, relationships of response—with things, trees, and animals. As Levinas writes, "The *ethical* aspects of the I-Thou relation, so frequently evoked in Buber's descriptions, are not determinant, and the I-Thou relation is also possible with respect to things."[26] And this is right. But this is also good.[27]

Despite his distaste for Buber's tree encounters, Levinas shows us how such a silent dialogue is conceivable: "One of the most interesting facets of Buber's thought consists in his attempt to show that the truth is not a content and that words cannot summarize it in any way; that it is more subjective, in a sense, than any other type of subjectivity; yet, as distinct from all purely idealist conceptions of the truth, it provides the only means of access to what is more objective than any other type of objectivity, i.e., to that which the subject can never possess since it is totally other."[28]

This insight (that an encounter is not understood through its content) occurs against the background of a confused reading of Buber, but philosophers rarely read each other well.[29] Levinas interprets Buber as contributing to a theory of knowledge, but he has an idiosyncratic notion of what this entails: "It leads us to original being. The subject has that function precisely because it is a subject of knowledge."[30] Here, Levinas departs from Buber's basic concern—understanding how I-You encounters differ from other encounters—and attempts to construct a philosophical anthropology out of *I and Thou*.[31] But the gist of Levinas's interpretation is that humans are constituted in and by "the between"; therefore, a human is not a constituting subject (he doesn't "make reality"). Instead, the meetings make us, which means we are beings of response, and *that* means the encounter is prior to content. The dialogue is more important than what we are talking about—after all, we may be talking about nothing. And it often is about nothing: Gossip, the weather, how you "are"—all are unimportant in relation to the dialogue in which they occur; the fact of the dialogue is what matters.

There is plenty to disagree with here, both with my reading of Levinas and Levinas's reading of Buber. But what Levinas gets right is that for Buber, encounter is prior to—and more important—than any content. This is why Buber can talk about silence that communicates, and it is also why dialogue with a silent plant might be more cogent than it seems at first. But plants are silent differently than we are. They also exist at a different tempo or, if you prefer, in a different temporality. Buber's encounter with the tree in *I and Thou* is an immediate encounter and still has something of the romantic revelation about it. However, domestic dialogue with plants can take place over years, punctuated by these encounters but not consisting of them.

Trees

Buber presents three descriptions of encountering a tree: in *Daniel*, *I and Thou*, and "Man and His Image Work." The importance of trees for Buber's understanding of dialogue is clearest in *Daniel*. Buber did not want *Daniel* translated into English because he thought it was undeveloped and abstract.[32] Indeed, the book revels in the abstract shape of presence, and a tree's shadow is enlisted to claim that an outline conveys more than the object itself: "Look at the ground, at the shadows of the trees as they stretch themselves over our path. Have you ever seen in the upper world of the trees a branch so outlined, so clear, so abstract as here? Is that not the branchness of the branch?"[33] Under the influence of Landauer, Buber will later reject this equation of essence (branchness) with abstraction (the shadow that shows an outline).

Nonetheless, in *Daniel*, we see a premonition of Buber's later work on dialogue. And, it is notable that a tree is where Buber first "sees" or, rather, touches, dialogue. "I pressed my stick against a trunk of an oak tree. Then I felt in twofold fashion my contact with being: here, where I held the stick, and there, where it touched the bark.... *At that time dialogue appeared to me* [*erschien mir das Gespräch*]. For the speech of man, wherever it is genuine speech, is like that stick; that means: truly directed address."³⁴

The situation is basically empty of interiority, communication, or signaling. In fact, it is barely an interaction: Everything seems to occur in Buber's head or his wooden phallus. This changes a few pages later, when the eponymous hero Daniel encounters another tree:

> Look at this stone pine. You may compare its properties with those of other stone pines, other trees, other plants.... And now seek to draw near to this stone pine itself. Not with the power of the feeling glance alone.... Rather, with all your directed power, receive the tree, surrender yourself to it. Until you feel its bark as your skin and the springing forth of a branch from the trunk like the striving in your muscles... until you are transformed. But also in the transformation your direction is with you, and through it you experience the tree so that you attain in it to the unity.³⁵

This example is more interesting as a *failure* to develop a dialogical relationship than anything else. Daniel's relation to the tree is one of absorption rather than conversation and reads more like consumption than encounter.³⁶ When Daniel says of his encounters, "The directed soul alone *rules* here," it's hard to interpret his transformation as much more than a human ego appropriating nature, spiritual tourism.³⁷ To paraphrase Huston, Daniel "absorbs" the tree by surrendering to it—but this is a "guided" surrender; Daniel remains firmly in control.³⁸

Daniel's relation to the tree is not "mysticism" in the sense of *uncontrolled* surrender, but neither is it dialogue.³⁹ By not surrendering the two participants remain separate, which is indeed a condition for dialogue. However, Buber avoids surrender, not to have an encounter but because it threatens his ego. When Daniel's interlocutor ("The Woman") suggests Daniel should have fully abandoned himself to the tree, Daniel replies that anyone who "surrenders" (*überantwortet*) to ecstasy is torn apart like Dionysus.⁴⁰ Fear of being torn apart governs the relationship to the tree: Buber wants the feeling of union without the disintegration that comes with it. So, independence is sustained out of fear, which is why Daniel feels "like" the tree, or "as" the tree feels. But the feelings are all too human, and the strangeness of tree-being is nowhere evident.

The tree is too passive to challenge the young Buber's "I."⁴¹ But as Buber matured he became more capable of formally reflecting on encounters with beings unlike himself. By the time he writes *I and Thou* (1923), he has a far more thoughtful and restrained description of what happens when you encounter a tree. Buber begins this passage with a list of things a tree encounter is not: It is not a picture; not a movement I feel, not a species I assign; not a function of scientific laws; and not a set of quantities or numeric relations. This list of what an encounter is not includes conflicting ways of sensing and understanding: quantitative and qualitative, aesthetic and scientific. Buber is not picking sides for or against mechanization or quantification—this is not Romantic.

What has changed is that Buber now knows encounters cannot be forced; you cannot make them happen by strength of personality alone:

> But it can also happen, if will and grace are joined, that as I contemplate the tree I am drawn into a relation, and the tree ceases to be an It. The power of exclusiveness has seized me.
>
> This does not require me to forego any of the modes of contemplation. There is nothing that I must not see in order to see, and there is no knowledge that I must forget....
>
> The tree is no impression, no play of my imagination, no aspect of a mood; *it confronts me bodily and has to deal with me as I must deal with it— only differently.*
>
> One should not try to dilute the *meaning* of the relation: relation is reciprocity [*Beziehung ist Gegenseitigkeit*].[42]

The combination of will and grace is an attempt, in theological language, to account for the fact that encounters cannot be willed because they are reciprocal. I cannot force the other being to encounter me, no matter how much I would like to. All I can do is prepare myself for them. Buber clarifies that this is not a question of "blinding yourself to see heaven"; there is no need to set aside scientific or artistic ways of encountering a tree. What is needed for this encounter is exclusiveness and reciprocity.

Buber bites the bullet when he claims meaning *is* reciprocity because this is precisely the part that is the hardest to accept. How can a tree possibly reciprocate? Here, the reciprocation concerns the situation, not the content of the situation. If we wanted the tree to communicate something to us as individuals, we would doom ourselves to nonsense. But Buber blocks this. Instead, the tree "confronts me bodily and has to deal with me as I must deal with it—only differently." How differently? "Does the tree then have consciousness, similar to our own? I have no experience of that. But thinking that you have brought this off in your own case, must you again divide the indivisible? What I encounter is neither the soul of a tree nor a dryad, but the tree itself."[43]

In terms of practice, Buber gives us little to work with. He says something like this: Look, it happened, you encountered a tree, and it encountered you. Accept that you have basically no idea how that happened. You've been lucky, that's all. On the one hand, this is not so different from any encounter with human beings; there, too, grace or luck is needed. On the other hand, "it's a mystery" is an annoying and disappointing response.

In the absence of content, the only thing left is the bare fact of reciprocity: The plant is, and the dialogue is. This is why it is with plants, even more than with God or gods, that Buber encounters the bare fact of reciprocity. In his 1957 afterword to *I and Thou*, Buber again returns to the claim that "it is part of our concept of the plant that it cannot react to our actions upon it, that it cannot 'reply.'"[44]

> Yet this does not mean that we meet with no reciprocity at all in this sphere. We find here not the deed of posture of an individual being but a reciprocity of being itself [*Reziprozität des Seins selber*]—a reciprocity that has nothing except being. The living wholeness and unity of a tree that *denies itself to the eye, no matter how keen, of anyone who merely investigates*, while it is manifest to those who say You, is present when they are present: they grant the tree the opportunity to manifest it, and now the tree that has being manifests it.

"The reciprocity of being itself" is what's left over when the tree is stripped of all particularity and content. It "is" the tree, the encounter, and nothing else. Here, the tree occupies a place close to God in Buber's thought; it exists at the threshold of the threshold and can be talked to, but not about.[45] It was not God, however, who confounded Buber's readers, but plants. They couldn't see how a reciprocal encounter with plant life is possible, and Buber provides very little help.

It is easier to explain how reciprocity with a tree is possible if we stop looking at a single encounter and turn our attention to dialogue. Dialogue requires less reciprocity in the moment because it happens at its own pace; it can ebb and flow. In 1955, in *Man and His Image Work*, we find a third, even more restrained, tree encounter. Buber mentions a linden he routinely passes and inquires about the tree when there is no one to sense it. What is the tree in the absence of correlation? If a tree grows in the forest and no one is around, what remains of the color green (which requires someone there to perceive it)? "For the green of the leaf . . . chlorophyll had to be substituted, and this, like . . . the biochemical findings about the life of the tree, drew me into the world of x where there existed only that which could not be realized."[46] Thinking or the tree in-itself or, rather, without-me, strips it of all relational content. All that remains is the "x": It is a tree without qualities.

This lack of specifics can be intolerable: "But I put up with it, I accepted the thing or unthing [*Unding*], which had become propertyless and uncanny, the thing that had waited for me in order to become once again the blooming and fragrant linden of my sense world. I said to the sense-deprived linden-x what Goethe said to the fully sensible rose: 'So it is you.'"[47]

This x, while unsensed, does not require us to leave aside sensation. It exists alongside the sensual, as the result of subtracting characteristics. The properties (like green, which is a relation between the tree and our eyes) disappear, and the tree grows uncanny. That a plant spurs Buber toward intuiting this "thing or unthing" should not surprise us: The strangeness of the plant helps us to think beyond the immediacy of the individual encounter.

With dialogue, we can go further than Buber. His concerns with "what happens in the moment I am there" and "what is left when I am not there" rankle only because encounter is all or nothing. But in our repetitive interactions with house plants—we need not be so bothered, because dialogue moves between latency and actuality. Dialogues can continue even if we check out for a while. But this is not enough to understand plant dialogue. How do we find any common ground with plants?

Irritability: Reciprocity and Worlds

Appeals to dialogue's leisurely pace do not rid us of the desire to understand how vegetal relationships are possible; indeed, these appeals *require* us to show how such relations are possible. With Jonas, Buber's concern with relationships is carried all the way down to the single cell, which helps us think about plant life in a dialogical sense. For Jonas, both biology and mind are made out of relationships. Life is relational because one of its fundamental characteristics is metabolism: counteracting entropy through the influx and outflow of energy and matter.[48] To be alive is to constantly add and expel, to stay afloat (until you don't). Mind is relational because all interpretation and "meaning" are part of a collective venture (if only through shared arbitrary symbol systems, like language).

There is no interiority-in-itself because the interior is developed out of relationships, even on a cellular level.[49] "Openness toward the world is basic to life. Its elementary evidence is the mere irritability, the sensitiveness to stimuli, which the simple cell displays as an integral aspect of its aliveness. *Irritability is the germ, and as it were the atom, of having a world,* just as the cell itself is the germ and the atom of the larger organism."[50]

Irritability and sensitivity are the beginning of a world insofar as they are indicative of *mediation*: To feel something is not the same as to be forced by something. To feel a push is not the same thing as to be pushed. I can feel pushed even when I am not being shoved, and a stone is pushed without feeling it. The Venus flytrap that shuts after having two hairs brushed by an insect doesn't sense individual insects, but it shows the beginnings of desire and relationship through its ability to sense and respond.

With "organic irritability as such . . . somehow already otherness, world, and object are germinally 'experienced,' that is, made subjective, and responded to."[51] We can easily exaggerate this and end up writing books about plants being people. The point is not that a plant has a world but that its sensorium provides the *beginning* of a world, the framework that will eventually allow the creation of shared worlds. the incredible gap created by language can fool us into thinking language is the origin of the world. However, in the beginning is not the word, but irritability—and plants are very irritable. Lacking the ability to discern objects—without a central nervous system—a plant's relationship to the world is one of sensitive surfaces: wide leaves, spreading roots, tendrils, all waiting for stimulation.[52] And while there is no "center" that a plant seeks to protect—its mechanisms are distributed across its body— it does protect its interior, in that plants sense, manage, and react.

Plants lack desire and motility. In Jonas's view, these two forces (movement and desire) are linked by the need to sustain an object while traversing a space. In simpler terms, a cat desires a mouse. It must keep track of the mouse and maintain its desire for the mouse, as it moves—at least until the mouse has been dispatched. Movement and desire are thus married: You move because you desire, you desire because you can move. Out of this desire grows the ability to view things as individuals and direct yourself toward objects.

Whereas the plant is rooted and therefore is "relieved of the necessity (as is also deprived of the possibility) of movement."[53] We should not lose sight of this: The plant is open to the world (and us, as part of this world), but its openness is not at all like ours, not just because of language but also because the structure of our desires is different. We may desire to be plantlike, or to vegetate, but this is rarely more than the desire to not desire because normal desires require that we *move*, or do things. And often, we just don't want to move.

Jonas gives us a way to think about plant relationships. Plants desire via irritation and relate via metabolism (at minimum) and nonlocomotive movement (like growth). A tree doesn't reciprocate feelings in a manner we understand, but it is in a reciprocal relationship with the world. However, we can go further without turning plants into effete versions of ourselves by asking about how plants interpret things.[54]

Living as a Form of Interpretation

A significant portion of modern Jewish philosophy is concerned with interpretation. The brief flourishings of interest in Jewish thought are almost always driven by this interest in interpretation. It is hermeneutics—not the ethical monotheism industrial complex—that Jewish thought contributes to larger discourses. But Jewish interpretive thought is often concerned exclusively with writing. The fact that most creatures don't read has led too many Jewish philosophers to ignore the natural world as uncomprehending and uninteresting. This is a mistake. It does not take much imagination to extend the concept of hermeneutics beyond the literate human (even if writing remains the focus of hermeneutics). Indeed, when Freud claims, "Psychoanalysis was above all an art of interpretation," he shows us a way interpretation can be extended to nontextual material realms (such as sex and shitting). It remains to show the converse, that some nontextual beings also interpret.

Jonas provides the notion that all living beings are engaged in reciprocal mediated processes, allowing us to consider plant life as being part of the semiotic world.[55] This is far more defensible than neo-Idealist claims such as Kohn's that "life is, through and through, the product of sign processes." It seems more prudent to say that life is *also* sign processes rather than a product of them.[56] Peirce's semiotics should allow us to better draw distinctions between different forms of life (à la Deacon) rather than to erase them (Kohn).

So, while we may speak of plants as interpreting beings, or as knowing things, we need to recognize the almost infinite distance separating how plants know and interpret from how we do. Plants know things, but as they have no nervous system, this knowing is very different from ours.[57] To even speak of *a* plant can be a problem because they are not individuated in the manner we are: "If the plant is not an organism consisting of interdependent organs, we should avoid conceiving it as a totality or as a differentiated whole."[58] And yet, we can say, "A head of lettuce has to know if there are ravenous aphids about to eat it up so that it can protect itself by making poisonous chemical. ... Cherry trees have to know when to flower," provided we don't assume a subject who knows.[59] This is admittedly a problem, and it explains why I'm not going to hang my hat on the claim that plants know things.[60]

The more important claim, that plants interpret the world, is far less a problem. It might seem strange to say interpretation is more basic than knowing, but we find instances of interpretation long before we find instances of knowing. At the very least, plant interpretation is more like our interpretation than plant knowing is like our knowing. While plant dialogue should not *depend* on the possibility that plants are junior hermeneuts, a shared hermeneutic ability can tell us *how* plant dialogue happens.

Here, Strathausen's unfortunately named book (*Bioaesthetics*) is an excellent guide.[61] Drawing from enactivism and theories of embodiment coming out of cognitive science, this book makes the sensible claim that "making sense is what organisms do throughout life to stay alive."[62] This is a refined version of Jonas's work on metabolism and mediation, suggesting that insofar as living beings are necessarily engaged in relationships, and these relationships require that creatures make sense of things, even at very basic levels, sense-making and interpretation are part of life. What we must give up for this is the assumption made by "traditional hermeneutics" that the "medium of language [is] the sine qua non of thought."[63] In other words, the (totally sympathetic) fear of the prelinguistic stands in the way of understanding nonhuman relationships and presents something of an Idealist trap. We should not be surprised that materialism is the dialogical position here, the position that has a place for life's paradoxes.[64] It is materially that we are fundamentally relational. It is as living material that we are wedded to death.

Is all of this merely to claim that plants, as living beings, are radically different from us but are still engaged in some of the same fundamental interpretive relationships and processes? Yes. When we are finished playing with the biologists, we return to Buber's living room.

Gardening and Time and Paying Attention

Plants have characteristics that shape our dialogues with them. Many of these are not shared. A sumac is like us because it is alive, but it is a very different form of life. The sumac may be alive, but it is a distributed life that lacks "depth"; it is not an individual in the animal sense, and neither does it recognize us as such; it occupies time differently. These differences are transformed by the domestic frame to cultivate a type of dialogue (not that I am suggesting anyone plant sumac near their houses). That plant life is dispersed or distributed is genuinely strange: If you pluck a flower, is it dead? Does it remain dead if you put it in water and it grows roots again? Where is the heart of a bush? What plant does a graft belong to? This affects how we relate to plants and their strange collectives. One can feel "inside" a forest, but it would sound strange to say you were inside a beach. Many of us crave encounters with this dispersed being because it helps us get in touch with our own distributed, nonindividual elements, even if only for a moment spent lying under a tree and losing ourselves in the leaf patterns (each of which is neither a self nor an organ).[65]

The garden transforms this notion. Plants seem (or even are) more individuated there. But this individuation is a one-way street. A plant in a garden seems like an individual for us in a way we are not for them. So it becomes easier for us to encounter a plant in a garden, but we cannot know if the converse is true (and I suspect it isn't). On its own, domestic space (the garden, the planter) is insufficient for plant dialogue; to this, we must add domestic time. This is the time of daily encounters, no matter how small and superficial. Yes, plants inhabit time differently, but living in the same space helps us bridge this gap, and this difference of tempo can end up being what binds us together.

Any home large enough brings together different tempos. A child's pace is different from a retiree's; a dog lives its entire life before you, often part of a series of dogs; plants move glacially. And yet our domestic interactions with plants can help us dialogue with a being that moves to a slow beat. Think of a time when you "killed a plant" because you did not feed it properly. Imagine this as being akin to one of Buber's miss-meetings—an encounter that is important precisely because it failed.[66] For Buber, such a missed encounter is often a necessary prelude to a real encounter.

Killing a plant—even the phrase invites responsibility—leads to a greater awareness of what a plant needs: that you must water it, check on it, that you can't just let it sit there like an object. Slowly, you develop habits around the plant; you get used to looking for signs it needs you, like wilted leaves; conversely, you need to learn not to over-meddle, to let the plant be. In time, you adjust your tempo to meet its tempo, and, if anything, this adjustment becomes part of your affection for the plant. This is the distinction between an I-You encounter and dialogue, this time of latency and intensity, learning to accept "moments" measured in inhuman terms. Dialogue's longer duration allows a different type of plant relationship and a more material form of reciprocity than the bare "reciprocity of being" because it stretches over time and is not an absolute moment, apophatic or otherwise.

When Buber meets his linden tree, the "x" behind the appearance, the "self" of the tree is completely mysterious. Things are different with dialogue. Mystery remains (as with every relationship worthy of the name), but it is attenuated and develops a shape. This is even clearer in the garden. Forgive the list, but there is a difference among growing beans (impersonal, used for food, short-lived), trying to get rhubarb to "take" (requires a gamble, takes a few years to know if it has worked), flowers (perennials, slowly growing, multiplying, it takes years to get them to look mature), fruit trees (prone to parasites, rusts, blight, in need of protection, you have to work to get them to mate), and so on. If a dialogical relationship is formed here, it is different in each case. I have never had much of a relationship with beans, but I am very attentive to the mood of the crab apple in front of my house.[67] Flowers, the most sexual of the household plants, develop aesthetic relations—aesthetics being another gateway for plant dialogues.[68]

A further note of caution is needed here: Not all reciprocal relationships are dialogical. Gardening doesn't magically bring you into communion with a pea plant. Too often, the *fact* of relationships is taken to mean that we are engaged in them. You and I are part of countless relationships we don't seriously engage with or take account of. Dialogue requires directedness toward your dialogue partner. It is true that dialogue can ebb and flow, but the relationship as a whole has to be permeated by our being directed toward the other being.

Plants complicate things because they don't reciprocate, nor are they directed toward us—not in any way comprehensible to us, at any rate. The house, like other places of practice, can cultivate this directedness, as do certain "monastic" forms of life, crafting, and educating.[69] The materially reciprocal relationship with a garden can retreat to the background and clear the way for privileged moments where the dialogue becomes more prominent and directed. But not all gardening does this. I was forced to garden as a child, and I guarantee that my resentful relationship with tomato plants was not dialogical.

It is easy to make fun of gardens, which Voltaire ruined as a place of retreat from reality. This, again, echoes the Attic notion of the house as privation. For Pangloss, after the world has kicked your ass you learn you are better off eating fruit in a garden. Candide refuses to learn any lessons and, like an idiot, repeats that we should tend "our" garden.[70] I have no idea if Voltaire meant gardening to be the battle cry of smug quietists, but that is what it has become, and it has given those with a phobia of the domestic an easy target.

The domestic garden further violates the supposed imperative that we must preserve the otherness of the other. Marder writes, "Whenever human beings encounter plants, two or more worlds (and temporalities) intersect: to accept this axiom is already to let plants maintain their otherness, respecting the uniqueness of their existence."[71] But is this really the case? In the garden, I slow myself somewhat to the plant's tempo and even try to see the world as it does. Letting the plant preserve its otherness is great for thinking—great for philosophy, but perhaps not so great for the garden and the dialogues it enables.

There is something of the fear of the domestic in these constant entreaties that we respect the otherness of the other, as if to do anything else would castrate them. This, of course, presupposes that I have the power to do damage to their otherness in the first place (the entreaty flatters us). The domestic is ideally a place where otherness is developed and cultivated, but for that very reason, it is also a place where we are brought closer to each other, whether we like it or not. The plant does not ask to be put in a garden any more than a child asks to be born into a life that will inevitably bring a great deal of suffering. And no one asks for chores.

Of course, even in the midst of gardening, we do not fully enter into plant temporality. But we do learn to "read" it. Just as plants interpret their environment, so we read plants, and we do so through a simple yet convoluted practice: by paying attention. Attentiveness is often a necessary prelude to dialogue and many other practices. Although Buber rarely treats attention with the level of precision we find in phenomenologists like Husserl, he is nonetheless a devotee, taking from Wundt (among others) the notion that attentiveness is the basis of freedom. To pay attention, not "to experience," but to give oneself over to the appearing of another creature is the ground for certain kinds of action that Buber favors. It is also the basis for dialogue when our partner is a creature of surfaces.

Buber flits from notion to notion to think about attention (*kavanah* or the direction of the heart in prayer, daydreaming, formation), and attention is both quotidian and fundamental for him. It is especially relevant to vegetal relationships. Taking a swipe at Heidegger, he writes, "The man who gazes without purpose on a tree is no less 'everyday' than the one who looks at a tree to learn which branch would make the best stick. The first way of looking belongs to the constitution of the 'everyday' no less than the second. (Besides, it can be shown that even genetically, in human development, the technical does not come first in time, and that what in its late form is called the aesthetic does not come second)."[72]

Here, the tree is let be, idly. Gardening, which is more of a means-end relationship, may not be quite so spiritual. However, as Buber noted about his father's agricultural pursuits, gardening is one of the best training grounds for attentiveness. It's not merely enjoyment; in gardening, we end up in the realm of symptoms and desires. Is a plant thirsty? Is it ill? What might begin as an attempt to master and control often ends up as something closer to vigilance or fascination.

However, a note of caution is in order.

Nonmutual Mutuality

Plant dialogues are the most difficult ones discussed in this book. More than any other type of dialogue, they run the risk of projection. Many people talk to plants, but flowers cannot hear and, in general, do not like to be touched. Additionally, these dispersed beings call into question our notion of the individual participant, depth, and mutuality, and they occupy time differently.

But this last difference is also part of what allows us to have dialogues—and not just encounters—with plants. The slow surfaces of the garden draw us into a dialogue that—because of its pace—allows us to see something like a plant's reactions, intentions, and desires. This is a place where dialogue is shown to be not some enervated I-You but actually a form of relation in its own right, one that can do things that encounter cannot.

5

BABIES

Noise and the Nursery

Babies are, in a literal sense, prelinguistic, as most of them are on their way to language. Loud and aggressive communicators, babies signal with indexes and icons, screams and cries, not words. Not all babies will develop into language, but (I assume) you and other readers of this book are ex-babies. This embarrassing fact might lead one to expect that baby dialogue would be easy for us, or at least easier than others discussed in this book: Although I have never been a cat or a tree, I have been a baby. But my previous job experience offers me little guidance. I have no recollection of being a baby, and my own infants were as foreign to me as were my cats. Perhaps more so. One of my cats lived with me for twenty-one years, whereas infancy is temporary; once you're used to it, it's gone.

The domestic rings circles around the baby: a series of enclosures, each around the last, slowly expanded as the baby ages, from birth into the bassinet, to the crib, to the bedroom, and further outward from there. Through much of the process we are treated to screams and cries at hours normally occupied only by sleep and hunger pangs. Fundamental relationships and a bizarre hermeneutics grow out of these wails and coos, watched over by a house stretched to breaking point by noise and exhaustion. The eventual entry into language is often viewed with equal parts joy and relief.

I wish to replace silence with crying as the exemplar of the prelinguistic. I want a much louder prelinguistic—not a silent communing, but bubbling noises, crying, and the other sounds of a nursery. Why are babies an exemplary instance of the prelinguistic, vis-à-vis dialogue? One hint is given by Anne O'Byrne: "There had to be at least one other present at our birth, not to mention the two that had to be there—or, given the state of reproductive technology, the at least two who had to exist or have existed somewhere—for our conception. Thus, when we select death as the cipher for our finitude and understand it as Heidegger did in *Being and Time*, it turns out to be what individuates us; birth, in contrast, reveals us as being in relation."[1]

Natality, birth, nursing, and early child-rearing are, if not dialogical, always plural: There is always more than one person there. We may all die alone, but our origins always involve others, and these others are usually very strongly imprinted on us. These relations can long outlive their members; after all, they are a matter of life and death: "As nothing stands between the child and destruction for the entire first year of his life except the tender care of his mother, we are not surprised if the maintenance of this maternal care begins to play a very important part in his life."[2] Quite.

As we focus on the specifics of baby dialogues and the ways they fasten themselves to us, we will rely on thinkers who were attentive to babies. Buber is no stranger to infants and their ways, but Freud and Melanie Klein join him to help us flesh out these earliest dialogues, half of which we no longer remember.

Because we forget the first few years of our life, we are reduced to rediscovering the life and world of a baby from the outside. As a record of these discoveries, Darwin's "Biographical Sketch of an Infant" is a delight. He spends little time trying to see things from the baby's point of view, instead recording small events that indicate the emergence of feelings and abilities. With infants, as with animals, Darwin sees activity and ability where others see passivity, hence his general position that "an infant understands to a certain extent, and as I believe at a very early period, the meaning or feelings of those who tend him, by the expression of their features."[3] We can dialogue with babies without assuming much about their abilities, but my claims are strengthened by the notion that babies communicate long before they possess the ability to manipulate arbitrary symbols. As Andrews writes, "Humans are born into the social cognitive domain": They orient toward faces at an extremely young age, and by ten months, they can "treat others as intentional agents" by doing such things as "engage in declarative pointing with adult caretakers, indicating objects of interest and checking to verify the partner's gaze."[4] The particulars of Andrews's survey need not concern us; what matters is that babies are communicating with indexical and iconic signs long before they can string together propositions. More important for our purposes are Andrews's claims that creatures can read *people* without reading words or minds. Babies can read a person's feelings and potential behaviors long before they can attribute a belief to that person. In other words, my son knew my dispositions long before he had a notion of me as a subject with specific beliefs.

I augment this claim with Melanie Klein's, which holds that babies can take objects and ascribe intention to them long before they can speak.[5] Indeed, Klein's work is nullified if this is not so. Her position (like Andrews's) helps us understand the shape of baby dialogues. These dialogues are like cat dialogues in that they involve a reasonably developed folk psychology and the taking of objects, but they are unlike cat dialogues in that they are part of the movement, or telos, out of babyhood into another form. When I talk to a cat, I am not trying to help it develop, nor do I expect the next dialogue to be radically different. A baby, however, is growing toward a very different type of being, and attentiveness to this process of transformation is often part of our baby dialogues.

Baby Talk

At first read it seems like Buber warps terms to exaggerate the importance of language, but this is complicated by the fact that Buber, for all his ground words, primal words, speech, and dialogue, can be quite dismissive of real existing language. Actual talk can weaken the dialogue by fixing things in the grid world and giving us an artificial sense of stability. Buber favors both bubbles and unstable encounters over the grid, so when language extends the grid and pops the bubbles, he gets ornery. So, on second read, it seems that Buber's use of grammatical concepts shrinks the importance of *actual* language: He is trying to articulate a relation that is language-like, and when actual language interferes with that relationship, it is dismissed.

Hence, his belief that presence need not involve any language whatsoever.[6] And yet Buber describes nonlinguistic relationships in dialogical terms, most notably the second-person stance, which sounds an awful lot like "language." That this has driven many to distraction, and others to abandon the project, is understandable and unsurprising. However, if we examine dialogue's more pedestrian elements, much of this potential confusion evaporates:

> Human dialogue, therefore, although it has its *distinctive life in the sign, that is in sound and gesture . . . can exist without the sign, but admittedly not in an objectively comprehensible form.* On the other hand an element of

communication, however inward, seems to belong to its essence. But in its highest moments dialogue reaches out even beyond these boundaries. It is completed outside contents, even the most personal, which are or can be communicated. Moreover it is completed not in some "mystical" event, but in one that is in the precise sense factual, thoroughly dovetailed into the common human world and the concrete time-sequence.[7]

Dialogue can be viewed as a series of overlapping layers, with signs giving it distinction, communication giving it personal import, and the most difficult to define layer "outside contents" being neither of these things.

Babies can help us here. While our dialogue with them may be completed outside of contents, babies produce a multitude of nonlinguistic gestures and signs that are, for all that, approaching language. They will not spare us the embarrassment of working with the prelinguistic, but they do spare us the embarrassment of pretending it's silent. So when Buber writes, "Only silence toward the You, the silence of all tongues, the taciturn waiting in the unformed, undifferentiated, prelinguistic [*vorzunglichen*] word leaves the You free and stands together with it in reserve where the spirit does not manifest itself but *is*," we are free to object.[8] Babies routinely scream their way through the most exalted encounters.

It is true that when someone presents something as "unmediated," we should be suspicious, because it's likely a swindle.[9] Buber's claim that "the relation to the You is unmediated" is troubling.[10] The problem worsens when he writes more expansively, "Before the immediacy of the relationship everything mediate becomes negligible."[11] The fact that some relationships—or moments—are unmediated is, for some, as intellectually offensive as Buber's insistence that we can talk to trees and animals, if not more so. Appeals to the unmediated are viewed by critical thinkers as masking an ideological move, and there are good reasons for their skepticism.

This is especially true when the unmediated object we are asked to "buy" is itself a mediating structure, as when the "economy" (the machine that carves up and mediates the world) is not itself subject to further mediation.[12] Acting as if these machines are basic and immediate is a con job and is why Derrida, one of the central figures in the fight against immediacy, is as critical of naive notions of structure as he is of unthinking invocations of presence, or signs.[13] Whether it's sex, economics, feeling, or beauty, all immediacy, including the prelinguistic, can be attempts to escape the machinations of critical thought and impose an unthinking order. Mediation is the basic machinery of critical thought, and to abandon it is dangerous. But is it always a mistake? Although the word *immediate* is a negation of *mediate* (and, therefore, at least for our words, mediation is prior to immediacy), one might ask *what* exactly is being mediated. The answer is frequently: another mediation. We have climbed the ladder out of immediacy into mediation, kicked away the ladder, and now everything is language, and, moreover, anyone who claims otherwise is a cynic or a fool.

The baby, of course, is a fool.[14] They are a problem for anyone who sees the linguistic subject as the quintessence of being human.[15] They are neither rational nor a subject (they cannot sign a contract), but, despite their most noble efforts, they are still a kind of human being.

The Mothers (Primordial Dialogue)

FAUST (startled). Mothers!
MEPHISTOPHELES. What? Afraid?
FAUST. The Mothers! "Mothers" sounds so strange!
MEPHISTO. And strange they are. No mortal knows these goddesses,
whom even we are loath to name.
You'll have to plumb the lowest depths to find their home,
but it's your fault we need their help.[16]

I and Thou includes several pages dedicated to a mythic scene where an emerging person moves from a prenatal relationship into an individuating infant. This scene, more than any other, shows how Buber conceived the primacy of relationships for human beings. It's important to dwell on this scene even though invocations of babies' perspectives are usually more ideological than thoughtful (and erase the existence of the mother).[17] That Buber had issues with his mother is obvious. That a fin de siècle Viennese thinker is likely to have some regressive thoughts about motherhood is also unsurprising.[18] But this episode shows us how and why Buber thinks relationships are prior to the things they relate.

Buber's genetic account works like this: Human beings emerge—*physically* emerge—within a prenatal relationship with their mother long before there is any notion of an individual "I" or objects. This is not a case of "first you have a fetus that then develops a relationship with its mother"; rather, the mother's body produces an internal relationship, one member of which slowly solidifies and then is expelled into the world, where it further seeks and develops relationships amid a domestic world full of relations.

The story of how this rupture occurs relies heavily on a notion of distancing. Distancing, like miss-meeting, is an attempt to explain the entry of the negative into the world, to explain how it is that distance and separation are real *things* for us and an essential part of what makes us human. Sure, the idea of the isolated or self-sufficient "I" might be a fantasy, but it's a real fantasy, and at the very least, it's worth asking how it is possible to have this fantasy in the first place. Even if one adopts a process metaphysics without discrete beings (just processes appearing as identities), daily human life depends as much on discreteness as it does on flow and flux. Humans not only discern discrete entities, but we also imagine and create them, which means we must be able to set things at a distance.[19]

Why? Because to have explicit relationships—relationships we can speak about—we need to conceive things and people as distinct from us. Buber, like Freud and Klein, assumes infants cannot initially tell the difference between themselves and their environment or between themselves and their mothers. Humans individuate through a long process, some elements of which can take decades. Buber's mature formulation of this concept is found in *Distance and Relation*, which postulates that humans can set themselves at a distance from objects and only *then* have discrete relationships over this distance. This and the notion of the in-between operate like a set of transcendental conditions for human beings: structures we assume to explain how we are possible.

Transcendental or not, Buber's story in *I and Thou* tries to give a material ground for our relationships, to show how distance and relation emerge out of the "basic" associations and separations of natural bodies: "The spiritual reality of the basic words emerges from a natural reality: that of the basic word I-You from a natural association [*naturhaften Verbundenheit*], that of the basic word I-It from a natural discreteness [*naturhaften Abgehobenheit*]."[20] These natural associations are derived from the fact of natality: "The prenatal [*vorgeburtliche*] life of the child is a pure natural association [*naturhaften Verbundenheit*], a flowing toward each other [*Zueinanderfließen*], a bodily reciprocity; and the life horizon of the developing being appears uniquely inscribed, and yet also not inscribed, in that of the being that carries it; for the womb in which it dwells is not solely that of the human mother."[21]

The notion that the womb is not solely the mother's will understandably raise eyebrows. Buber's goal is not to infringe on reproductive health but to show that the preborn exist in a strange in-between state. He does not posit the child as in-between the two parents, as one might expect. Such a move would place the emerging person inside a community, though a small one, as the "dash" between the mother and the father. Instead, the person emerges from an inchoate relationship in the womb.

The desire and need for relation thus begins in utero, where we are a product of the relation, and the relationship—literally and biologically—sustains us (before we have even the crudest notion of the "I" or self). Like psychoanalysis, Buber looks to the material facts of natality and prenatality to explain our desire for certain relationships.[22] Where cruder forms of psychoanalysis claim that this desire is escapist, Buber insists this our desire to be in relationships is not "return to the womb" escapism.[23] The desire is not to be re-enclosed; the desire is for the reciprocal, with prenatal life being the first and most physical form of reciprocity. Buber thus claims that the material process of human development begins in and tends toward relation.

Human infants spend a remarkably long time developing the most basic level of awareness. Buber gathers these experiences under the troubling rubric of the "great mother" in order to claim that relation is prior to the related objects:

> Every developing human child rests, like all developing beings, in the womb of the great mother—the undifferentiated, not yet formed primal world [*vorgestalitigen Urwelt*]. From this it detaches [*löst*] itself to enter a personal life, and it is only in dark hours when we slip out of this again (as happens even to the healthy, night after night) that we are close to her again. But this detachment [*Ablösung*] is not sudden and catastrophic like that from the bodily mother. The human child is granted some time to exchange the natural association with the world that is slipping away for a spiritual association—a relationship . . . the child lives between sleep and sleep (and a large part of waking is still sleep).[24]

The Goethean "great mother" indicates the distance of Buber's genesis story from a properly biological one. This mother is never left once and for all, as the process of detachment is never completed—some trace is retained, at least in the ego dissolution that accompanies sleep.

In plainer language: Throughout infancy humans establish independent objects, a process that reaches completion with the acquisition of language (which concretizes distinctness by giving things names). This process is gradual. You begin in a state of pure association (where the difference between me and other things isn't clear) and end up in a world where things have outlines and names. Buber insists that some trace of the earlier phases of association remains with us, if only in dreams. This is why he can say there is something a priori about the structure of the "You." There is always a chance to return from dissociation or alienation to a "natural association" with the great mother (if not, perhaps, your real mother).

Sloterdijk, in his somewhat humorous writing on "negative gynaecology," argues that the essence of great mother stories is a longing for a relationship that is not based on objects. If relation begins before we are outside the womb, then our basic relations are not to identifiable objects but to intimate, or "placental," ones.[25] The continual reentry into the space of indeterminate intimacy (where it is unclear what is I and what is You) establishes a connection between the preobject relation and distinct relations.[26]

After birth, the child enters a new womb-like space, often domestic. This place (hopefully) shelters the child as it develops from "natural association" to a broader set of social associations. The home and the family ideally play a mediating role between the womb and the world, which in part explains the womb-like image of the house enclosure. For Buber, this development is more evidence that we are born with the drive for relations, a drive that is developed, rather than viewing the relationship drive as something we come to later in time:

> The innateness of the longing for relation is apparent even in the earliest and dimmest stage. *Before any particulars can be perceived*, dull glances push into the unclear space toward the indefinite; and at times when there is obviously no desire for nourishment, soft projections of the hands reach, aimlessly to all appearances, into the empty air toward the indefinite . . . this motion will gain its sensuous form and definiteness in contact with a shaggy toy bear and eventually apprehend lovingly and unforgettably a complete body: . . . coming to grips with a living, active being that confronts us, if only in our "imagination."[27]

Buber's infant is as close as we can get to a human with no notion of other beings, who is yet hungry for relationships. Having just emerged from a relationship where the (m)other is seemingly all and everything (and so, not a thing), the infant wants relations (but not to a thing). That Klein presents a more material, object-centered story—one with real mothers—is as obvious as it will be helpful, but her story is not as different from Buber's as one might think. Both are interested in the drive to relations with partial objects, meaning objects not conceived of as independent or self-sufficient.

Buber's story stops short of spiritual claims and rests in the more respectable land of imagination. *Imagination* and *fantasy* are tricky terms, and Buber does not provide definitions. I place him in the lineage of

Judeo-Arabic philosophy, where imagination is a form of thinking, one that supplies the missing pieces to reason and sensation. In other words, fantasy is not necessarily a falsehood; it is a way of filling out an image, much like I "fill out" the parts of an object I cannot see. The infant touches a toy and imagines it as a living being. But what does this imply—that the child is an idiot? Perhaps. But also that the structure of its first postulations is relational, that its imagination is already looking for company, and that it is building partners even where none are to be found.

That this is a fantasy does not mean its structure is incorrect. Some fantasies accord with very real mechanisms, as Buber thinks this one does: "This 'imagination' [*Phantasie*] is by no means a form of 'panpsychism' [n.b., *Allbeseelung* not *Panpsychismus*]; it is the drive to turn everything into a You, the drive to pan-relation; and where it does not find a living, active being that confronts it but only an image or symbol of that, it supplies the living activity from its own fullness."[28]

What is supplied by the child? The belief that the encounter is with something real. What does this suggest? It doesn't mean that the child's universe is made of mind or life; rather, it suggests something cruder: The child imagines a relationship with everything. The child's mind is relationship-ready and is willing to fill in the needed pieces where its very limited sensation or cognition cannot.

This drive for relation reaches an important milestone with speech. As Buber puts it, "Little inarticulate sounds still ring out senselessly and persistently into the nothing; but one day they will have turned imperceptibly into a conversation—with what? Perhaps with a bubbling tea kettle, but into a conversation [*Gespräch*]. Many a motion that is called a reflex is a sturdy trowel for the person building up his world. It is not as if a child first saw an object and then entered into some relationship with that."[29]

Before an infant develops an aptitude for arbitrary symbols, they are already trying to have a conversation. My daughter would spend up to half an hour trying to talk to a duck with a poorly emulated *quack* long before she was able to use proper words. First, we have the longing (or desire), then we have an inchoate otherness—a "wordless anticipation of saying You," and only later do we have notions such as the "I" or a "thing." Each step is part of a separation, or distinction, from the initial state of relation, but each step is also a reparation and acknowledgment of this separation: The further the infant moves from its initial state of indefinite reciprocity, the more it is able to articulate it.

Buber claims that dialogue with infants is possible and further provides a story to explain why we desire dialogue to begin with. His myth presents us with a permanent drive for relation, dialogue being one of the chief forms this can take. Melanie Klein (literally) fleshes this out for us and provides a more materialist story of infant development—and objects will appear even earlier. Buber's myth has philosophical implications, but Melanie Klein's more physical (and violent) story—and, even more, her method—ventures into realms Buber has overlooked.

Melanie Klein: Objects Before Language

At the age of 32 days he perceived his mother's bosom when three or four inches from it, as was shown by the protrusion of his lips and his eyes becoming fixed; but I much doubt whether this had any connection with vision.[30]

—*Charles Darwin*

More than any other object discussed in this book, with the possible exception of plants, the baby is a mercurial creature. After even a day apart, one returns to a slightly different infant.[31] An infant's unstable nature—swinging from a plantlike immobility to an effervescent locomotion—comes with constantly changing openings to dialogue. Any discussion of infant dialogue should address development.

Melanie Klein, the preeminent theorist of both breastfeeding and play therapy, can guide us here.[32] Her writings on infancy are among the best entries in the canon of modern Jewish thought—and, perhaps, any European thought—on children and their relations. Fixing her firmly in the canon would take us far afield, and while her mother came from a line of cultured Slovakian rabbis (and her father from a Polish Jewish family), she shared Freud's scorn for religion of all forms. She summarized her relationship to Jewishness in her occasionally tendentious autobiography: "Another thing I have always hated was that some Jews, quite irrespective of their religious principles, were ashamed of their Jewish origin, and, whenever the question arose, I was glad to confirm my own Jewish origin, though I am afraid I have no religious beliefs whatever."[33] Regardless of one's position on Klein's canonical status, I suggest her work provides a useful, if not necessary, supplement.

For instance, Klein allows us to more seriously consider infant dialogue than even Freud does. In this one regard, she takes Freud more seriously than he takes himself: "One of the most fundamental and far-reaching discoveries ever made in human history was Freud's finding that there exists an unconscious part of the mind and that the nucleus of this unconscious mind is developed in earliest infancy."[34] Klein takes Freud's investment in childhood and runs with it: She moves earlier in time, focusing attention on the infant's earlier stages, and, of more importance for us, she analyzes infants themselves. This is her central virtue for the present project: not that she assigns infanthood more importance than Freud, but that she spends more time with the thing itself.

This requires two basic transformations of psychoanalysis (for which she has still not been forgiven). The first is a centering of the mother. Assuming standard gendered parental roles (as both Klein and Freud did), the age of the child matters very much here. Freud, more interested in children after they began to speak, can thus write "I cannot think of any need in childhood as strong as the need for a father's protection."[35] But Klein's interest in the infant begins with birth and the first feeding. Thus, it is the mother and her breast that take center stage for Klein's infant. The second transformation concerns language. While Freud's position on infancy and language can be debated, Klein's cannot. Her project depends on the notion that infants can have complex relationships with objects long before they begin to speak actual language.

As Kristeva writes, "While the Freudian unconscious is structured by desire and repression, Melanie Klein focused on the newborn's psychic pain, on his splitting processes, and on his early capacity for a rather limited form of sublimation. The Freudian drive has a source and an aim, but no object, while in Klein's view, the newborn's drives are directed from the outset toward an object (the breast or the mother). In Klein's world, the Other is always already there."[36]

Klein, far less formally educated than many of her Viennese peers, was relatively uninterested in the interpretation of Freud's texts and instead focused her hermeneutic efforts on infants themselves. Her brutal style allowed her to break with nascent pieties while remaining within the psychoanalytic fold. She has forever gained the contempt of those who think that psychoanalysis cannot function without language, and is resented by those who are annoyed that the breast displaces the phallus as the fundamental object.[37] We, however, who wish only to use Klein's insights and methods to think about infant dialogue, do not need to take a position in psychoanalysis' internecine conflicts.[38]

Breasts and Toys

There is a cliché in computer design that "the only intuitive interface is the nipple." It's not clear who first said this but it is absolute nonsense. The nipple may well be intuitive for nonhumans, but breastfeeding is often extremely difficult for mothers and babies alike. The infant's frustration *with the very thing that keeps it alive* is, for Klein, the reason the breast is the ur-object, the thing divided against itself, the unification of which is closely tied to the infant's development of an ego.[39] The breast (or bottle) is the infant's first object, not the mother, who comes later.

As Klein puts it in a mature work:

> I have often expressed my view that object-relations exist from the beginning of life, the first object being the mother's breast which to the child becomes split into a good (gratifying) and bad (frustrating) breast; this splitting results in a severance of love and hate. I have further suggested that the relation to the first object implies its introjection and projection, and thus from the beginning object-relations are moulded by an interaction . . . between internal and external objects and situations. These processes participate in the building up of the ego and superego and prepare the ground for the onset of the Oedipus complex in the second half of the first year.[40]

For Klein, the splitting of the breast is almost as important as the breast itself. What does this mean? It means that sometimes, a thing appears that sates the hungry infant, which is the good breast. But sometimes, when it is hungry, another thing arrives, which taunts the infant and delivers nothing, or stands away from it, and this is the bad breast. The baby loves the good breast and despises the bad, longs for the first and seeks to destroy the second. With time, the baby realizes the two breasts are in fact the same thing, which can create a crisis. The baby's desire to destroy the bad breast also destroys the good, and so the baby seeks to repair it.

With the breast, the negative enters the world, and it does so via activity, not language. As Eva Brann notes in her work on negation, children don't usually negate things in language until quite late (usually by saying no, after about eighteen months or so).[41] But they destroy things much earlier. The breast is not a light switch, flicked on and off by an angry little deity. Rather, the child imagines, or enacts, tearing the mother, or her breast, apart. Babies long for relations, destroy them, and then anxiously repair them: "If the baby has, in his aggressive phantasies, injured his mother by biting and tearing her up, he may soon build up fantasies that he is putting the bits together and repairing her. This making reparation is, in my view, a fundamental element in love and in all human relationships."[42] This secularized tikkun olam (repairing the world) is prelinguistic, as are, in turn, all desires to destroy and mend, to alienate and connect—which are to be carried into the linguistic world by confused subjects.

The material elements of this process are detailed in Klein's early *Weaning* (1936). She begins by noting that "the first gratification which the child derives from the external world is . . . being fed"—the infant has no object, just an outside, or "world." Eating is no simple matter of satisfying hunger. It is claimed that the baby finds pleasure "when his mouth is stimulated by sucking at his mother's breast. This gratification is an essential part of the child's sexuality, and . . . its initial expression. Pleasure is experienced also when the warm stream of milk runs down the throat and fills the stomach."[43] Feeding is an immersive experience, and the baby quickly develops its first object: its mother's breast (not the mother "as a person" or object).

But this is complicated. The baby also experiences frustration and reacts with rage. "These feelings of hatred are directed towards the same objects as are the pleasurable ones, namely, the breasts of the mother." Out of these two rather different feelings and relationships, the infant begins, as Buber notes, to build its first fantasies, to complete objects in its imagination (as it cannot sense them). Klein is convinced that babies begin to develop figures and fantasies "almost from birth" and that these are directed at their mother's breast. She admits it "may seem curious that the tiny child's interest should be limited to a part of a person rather than to the whole, but . . . the child has an extremely undeveloped capacity for *perception*."[44] A newborn can perceive almost nothing; its entire sensorium is committed to the seemingly simple act of feeding, so every minor element takes on sublime importance.

From here, Klein develops her work. The good breast is the prototype of the good, the bad breast of persecution and evil; projection and introjection begin, and the child is on its way. Of concern to us is the development of the ego, as Klein's "I," like Buber's, is developed in relationship to an other. But as we have seen, the other is only part of a person, a partial object, which is split into an angelic and demonic side. As the baby matures, its sensorium expands and objects take on permanence; the two breasts are slowly integrated into one, as is the child's ego.[45] "The mother's breast, both in its good and bad aspects, also seems to merge for him with her bodily presence; and the relation to her as a person is thus gradually built up from the earliest stage onwards."[46] And so on until the baby can perceive and conceive the mother as a person and, in time, come to the terrifying realization that its mother does not belong to the baby alone.[47]

Why is this of interest to us? Klein tells a story not unlike Buber's in which the child moves into a state where it can take an object, say "You," and have a relationship. And like in Buber's story, the development of the "I" and the development of the "You" or "It" proceed in lockstep with the expansion and integration of its relationships. Of course, this process is hardly universal. Klein, hunting for pathologies, is well aware that there are deviations from this script.

This process, as described by Klein, is not merely preparatory for dialogue but already contains a strong dialogical element: a slow-moving alteration between presence and absence based on a relationship that is reciprocal (if extremely asymmetrical). Here, some questions arise: Is breastfeeding dialogue, and is it a dialogue that helps form and frame later dialogues? Cooking and eating are not merely a space where dialogue is cultivated, but they can themselves be a form of conversation. Yes, to say "Cooking is my love language" is a horrific cliché, but the cliché chosen is "language" for good reason. Perhaps it's special pleading, but I have long sought to communicate my affection for friends and family through cooking, in what is perhaps a very distant echo of this more formative maternal practice.

Is breastfeeding dialogue? Is cooking? We have left the great mothers and arrived at an actual mother, and the result is no less mysterious or important. On the contrary.

Play

Play is the exultation of the possible.[48]

—Martin Buber

How do you dialogue with a baby when feeding isn't an option? Melanie Klein could hardly feed all her tiny analysands: The obstacles to psychoanalysis are similar to those facing dialogue; namely, babies don't speak but are on their way to language. Klein's "solution" or, rather, her method, is disarmingly simple: play. Klein played with her analysands, which is a relationship that can be directed toward other relationships, all without needing language (but having space for it, when the child learns to talk).

Later in life, Klein wrote "Some Theoretical Conclusions Regarding the Emotional Life of the Infant," in which she claimed, "My work with both children and adults, and my contributions to psychoanalytic theory as a whole, derive ultimately from the play technique evolved with young children."[49] A strong statement, but one borne out by a reading of her work. Play was done with small nonmechanical toys that symbolized as little as possible (for instance, there were no toys that suggested an occupation). They were laid out for the child and analyst to play with.[50] Simplicity was the watchword: "Their very simplicity enables the child to use them in many different situations, according to the material coming up in his play." This environment is less controlled than the classic couch and chair setup: children could bring in their own objects, and the games follow the child's lead.

Klein's play therapy was largely a matter of practice rather than theory, so the details of her play-work are hidden in her notes and recordings rather than her published work. Susan Sherwin-White has used these sources to demonstrate that, for Klein, play was the widest pathway to understanding a baby's preverbal "language" and so to discover its anxieties, terrors, and desires.[51] Play is potentially dialogical and allows for directedness toward one's partner, but it can also be "about" things and, in turn, allow relationships to other objects. A stick turned into a phone can draw attention in many directions: toward the watching parent, an imaginary caller, and, just as often, to the "phone" itself. The stick both is and is not itself, and the relationships opened by play similarly allow for a back-and-forth between directed presence and an expression of something otherwise missing from the situation.

To define play is itself a book. From Huizinga onward the humanities have flirted with play, even making it an ideology of sorts. The danger with play is that when we talk about it, it generally seems "good" and lighthearted. But, as Nietzsche (among others) has noted, play can be deadly serious. Interrupt a child playing and see a flash of violence. Conversely, one might turn matters of life and death into "games," if only to maintain sanity. Klein's play therapy is not intended to valorize play; rather, it uses it as a form of prelinguistic communication. For us, it provides a substructure for dialogue.

Anthropological, ethnological, and philosophical work on play is extensive; we suffer from an embarrassment of riches. Even the most cursory readings suggest that play is and is not human. Gadamer expresses this nicely: "It is obviously not correct to say that animals too play, nor is it correct to say that, metaphorically speaking, water and light play as well.

Rather, on the contrary, we can say that man too plays. His playing too is a natural process."[52] Infants play before language, and this presubjective element of play is sustained in later playing. In other words, play doesn't require subjects, and part of the reason play is delightful is that it allows us to leave identity behind for a moment.[53] Play opens the door to a hermeneutics without an "I" or a written text.

Klein instrumentalizes play insofar as it has a function: to discern an infant's relationships and desires. We, however, are free to simply play. But let's get quotidian: Much of parenting is not about satisfying a baby's needs, but discerning them. The pre-Lacanian question (What does baby want?) is pressing because infants cannot speak. Play assumes babies enter into relationships, but it is also the point at which one can *see* the manipulation of relations (and relations of manipulation) without symbolic content.[54]

For Klein, play was not a departure from psychoanalysis, but its fulfillment, not only because of the investment in childhood but also because it "corresponds to a fundamental principle of psychoanalysis—free association. In interpreting not only the child's words but also his activities with his toys, I applied this basic principle to the mind of the child, whose play and varied activities . . . are means of expressing what the adult expresses predominantly by words."[55] Toys are, of course, objects, not words, and as objects, they often accrue greater emotional investments than words do.[56] For instance, as Klein notes, the attitude children take toward toys they have damaged can be "very revealing."[57] Playing with toys remains language-like: A toy can easily represent something it is not; it has moved between players, and with it, a shared world is built.

Building Bubbles for the God of Noise

Our brief excursion through the criminally neglected work of Melanie Klein is an invitation to dinner and not the meal itself. Infants are important for materialist elements of modern Jewish thought, most obviously, Buber, Klein, and Freud but, arguably, Benjamin and Jonas as well. The reasons for this are different in each case, but two come to mind: Studying the development of a human helps rid us of Idealist fantasies where the complete adult mind is the basic unit for thinking, and more importantly for this volume, the infant provides an example of the prelinguistic that is not a Romantic escape from language but rather its precursor.

I have known people, real people, who believe you can talk to God, but who do not extend the same courtesy to babies. I understand: Babies are loud, chaotic, and often disgusting. Darwin again:

> The noise of crying or rather of squalling, as no tears are shed for a long time, is of course uttered in an instinctive manner, but serves to show that there is suffering.... Moreover, he appeared soon to learn to begin crying voluntarily, or to wrinkle his face in the manner proper to the occasion, so as to show that he wanted something. When 46 days old, he first made little noises without any meaning to please himself, and these soon became varied. An incipient laugh was observed on the 113th day, but much earlier in another infant. At this date I thought, as already remarked, that he began to try to imitate sounds, as he certainly did at a considerably later period. When five and a half months old, he uttered an articulate sound "da" but without any meaning attached to it. When a little over a year old, he used gestures.[58]

The expressive does not thrum and pulse like the divine spheres; rather, it spits and wails. Babies take up inside our walls and pull us into inhuman dialogues through play and feeding. With babies, more than any other being discussed, the domestic sphere is essential to cultivating dialogue; without some form of it, the baby is likely to die. So, we build and reinforce the domus to hold the baby as it moves toward language and locomotion. These little gods of noise can easily destroy a home, and so broader circles (family, neighbors, friends) often come to help maintain the space for the first period after birth.

Ideally, we can give these monsters a place of stability, creating a world that does not move apace with the vortex of becoming that rages in the streets. The domestic, seen from the perspective of dialogue, provides a space that is stable but lacks the repression we associate with stability. Stability is needed because "a child needs what is constant, what is dependable. There must be something there that does not fail."[59] As Buber puts it in a work on children and education: "He is educated by the elements, by air and light and the life of plants and animals, and he is educated by relationships. The true educator ... must be to the child as one of the elements."[60] For Klein, babies need to be protected from the world's prohibitions, and so her proposal is even more radical than Buber's: "The irrefutable conclusions to be drawn from psycho-analytic experience demand that children shall whenever possible be protected from any over-strong repression.... We can spare the child unnecessary repression by freeing—and first and foremost in ourselves—the whole wide sphere of sexuality from the dense veils of secrecy, falsehood and danger spun by a hypocritical civilization upon an affective and uninformed foundation."[61]

Both Buber and Klein require that we change ourselves. At the risk of drawing together threads that belong apart, for the prelinguistic infant, the domestic combines the need for stability and feeding with the an-arche of play. This combination is unsustainable, but so, too, is infancy.

6

SENSUALITY
Tools, Crafts, Decoration

I've made it easy on myself by sticking to living beings. This is because life can be thought of as engaging in reciprocal, hermeneutic relationships. Even if these relationships are strange, it's not too difficult to see how we can join them. But nonliving beings? "Dead" matter? Even this latter term is too much—a stone is not even dead. And yet our relationships with nonliving things (or "mere things"—tone matters here) can be dialogical: pianos, knives, chisels, cars, banisters, pens, laptops, and so on. These things, even manufactured things, can enter reciprocal relationships.

In this final chapter I explore sensuality, which is our gateway into the material world, the world of things. Why sensuality? Because Buber's theory of sensuality goes a long way toward explaining how it is that we can dialogue, in theory, with *anything* we are aware of. Art and crafting will be our guide. For Buber, crafting is an intensified sensuality, so exploring craft will help illustrate his theory of sensation. Finally, we will note a significant distinction between dialogue and the I-You: Dialogue is often more mediated and sensual than an immediate relationship of presence; dialogue does not oppose instrumental relationships, so much as work with them. To understand this, we will examine the tools we use to craft things. Tools allow us to see dialogue within instrumental relationships and challenge the cliché that we shouldn't treat people like things.

Objects fill houses. Relationships are developed with some of them; others are merely functional. Some people have a penchant for handcrafted things which have been humanized by the marks of their labor. Romantics seem to like broken things; stripped of their functionality, they become easier to relate to. I am partial to gifts, souvenirs, and things that recall a place. What I mostly see, however, is affection for things that have been owned for a long time—long enough that even their glitches and hiccups are soothing and seem to individuate us and the tool. Musical instruments are almost too obvious an example; with few exceptions, anyone who has played an instrument for more than a few years can speak of a relationship with it.

Our day-to-day language confuses things. When I use a person to satisfy my needs, we say I am treating them "like a thing." But when I relate to a thing in a reciprocal manner, nobody says that I am treating it "like a person." This confusion between our intentional stance and the object's agency has generated a flood of works that try to overcome death by declaring everything alive, moving, and engaged. That is not this chapter's strategy; rather, its more modest goal is to understand how we can relate to the nonliving and dead things that populate our houses.[1] We do this by exploring crafting, the act of making and decorating things—not because crafting is our primary relationship with things but because it is one of the easiest relationships to understand. Crafting leaves physical traces and effects that record our interaction, so to speak.

Besides being somewhat easy to understand, crafting also exemplifies a fundamental type of relationship: sensuality. By showing how crafting dialogues occur, we will see why Buber thinks we can dialogue with anything. To reveal the plot: The reason we can do this is that the structure of sensation and awareness are already dialogue-like.

Here, as elsewhere, reciprocation is the bullet we must not dodge. It is hard to see how I can dialogue with nonliving beings because it is hard to see how they could possibly reciprocate. And if reciprocation is founded in cognition or will, then they don't. But Buber suggests another possibility for reciprocity. When Buber writes that "the limits of the possibility of dialogue are the limits of awareness [*Innewerdens*]," we must take him quite literally: If you can be aware of it, you can dialogue with it.[2] This is because awareness has a potentially dialogical element. This chapter limits itself to only one form of awareness: sensation. If we adopt the basics of Buber's theory of perception, if we view sensation as a relationship between the sensed and the sensor, then dialogue is always possible. Possible, mind you, not usual: Only a tiny number of sensual relationships are also dialogical.

If we view sensation as a dynamic relationship with an object, as a "back and forth" or "meeting" between us and an object ("x"), a door is opened through which dialogue can enter. Viewing sensuality in this way creates a foundation for dialogue. Crafting is a refined and tangible form of this sensuality because it shapes sensual relationships and leaves an object in its path. It is a material instance of dialogue with nonliving beings.

Art

Buber's first thoughts on perception, sensation, and craft are found in his early works on art. It's a mere accident of history that Buber did not end up an art historian. As Zachary Braiterman has shown, these works exhibit theories of form and creation that Buber never abandons.[3] However, these formal aesthetic principles are easily hidden by their goal, as these early works are intended to bolster a Jewish renewal through cultural Zionism, not to establish a philosophy of art or *Gestalt* for its own sake. Jewish art was to serve a Jewish Renaissance, which was in turn to help Jews develop a more "complete world view." This renaissance was intended to reestablish deeper thing-relationships with "heart and nature . . . trees, birds, and stars," but the specific nature of these relations was unexplored. Instead, it is merely postulated that these relationships are important and denied to Jews under the condition of exile.[4]

However, no matter their political role, the early writings initiate a long-standing concern with form and formation, which eventually plays a role in Buber's philosophy of dialogue.

In particular, Buber's readings of specific artists, such as Lesser Ury or Michelangelo, demonstrate an early interest in the role of movement, sensation, and formation in the artist's craft, even before Buber was committed to principles of *Gestalt*.[5] Of equal interest for us is that the specific art form Buber focused on and favored—Jugendstil or art nouveau—was craftwork-adjacent.[6] And his explicit model for Jewish renewal was the Arts and Crafts movement, with its emphasis on handiwork and overcoming alienation through craft.[7]

So when Buber denies the possibility of Jewish art in his day because "national art needs soil from which to develop and a heaven toward which to flow," he doesn't mean that Jews aren't creating art or even that they aren't making art as Jews. He means that there is no *national* art.[8] Indeed, his project requires that there be already existing types of creativity that create forms that will guide and be incorporated into the emerging nation. This is why, in the very piece where Buber denies the existence of Jewish art, he nonetheless lauds Lesser Ury for creating a new *language*.[9] Ury's new language is one of color, not form, because at this early stage, Buber actively dislikes form. The young Buber thinks of form as cut off defined by its outline. And so form is antidialogue: "Form does not say anything about reciprocal relations, the reciprocity of things. But this is the essential. The thing is nothing in itself. . . . Close it off and you kill it. The most personal rests in the relationship to the other."[10] For Buber, Ury's value is in large part the creation of a language of relationships that opens up closed forms to other beings.

And so, we find ourselves back in Buber's three spheres. While I have mostly focused on the first sphere (nature) and ignored the second one (humans), here, it is the third sphere (spiritual beings) that is important. Spiritual beings [*geistigen Wesenheiten*] are not magical; rather, they are works of art, culture, and religious formations (including *images* of God).[11] As Buber writes in *I and Thou*, life with spiritual beings, or works of art, "*lacks but creates language . . .* we hear no You and yet feel addressed."[12] As noted previously, spheres 1 and 3, nature and spirit, share a secret connection because they lie outside of language. For both, dialogue occurs without words.

In spheres 1 and 3, dialogue—when it is to have a medium at all—needs a medium other than language. With Ury, the medium is painting, but underlying this is movement. Why movement? Because—in this early work, at least—Buber sees movement as a creative relationship of construction and destruction where permeable bodies affect each other, as opposed to form, which is a closed shape, a nonrelational prison. Ury uses color to express movement's relation, which in turn is grounded in a pantheism where everything is connected. But Ury's pantheism "is not harmonious pantheism, perhaps a cyclopslike pantheism. It is a pantheism of storm, of movement."[13] This storm "creates a language" in color, which in turn is meant to express a world where "natura naturans [the creative element of nature] is everywhere, in me, in you, from me to you, from you to me."[14]

Motion

The importance of motion is constant for Buber, from his earliest writings on art to his final writings on anthropology and images. Here, I move between his "Lesser Ury" (1903) and one of his last pieces, the inimitable "Man and His Image Work" (1955). This second piece is explicitly a work of anthropology, meaning an account of the human element in art. The piece's title references Genesis 1:27: "And God created man in His own image"—only to draw a near-total distinction between the biblical account of God's creation and our own making and crafting (a distinction discussed in the next section). For now, it suffices to note that no matter one's view on the "unformed and void," God's creation is "independent of all otherness," whereas human beings are absolutely dependent on other beings for our existence, and our creations reflect this.[15]

For Buber, the question of art—especially the creation of art—begins with "the human senses."[16] Why? Because sensuality is where our dependence on the existing world asserts itself. Sensation is where we encounter things that do not depend on us, the materials of life. In the sense world, "the dependence of man on the existent properly constitutes itself and that which determines the reality-character of all art . . . *no mental and no emotional element may enter into art otherwise than through becoming a thing of the senses.*"[17] Sensation is the reality principle for art, the place where we bump into what we are not, and sometimes this encounter is a dialogue.

Buber's post-Kantian model for sensation has several affinities with contemporary models of embodied and extended cognition. Sensation is explicitly extended and embodied because sensual relationships between us and the world are constituted by movements: "There is no movement that is not directly or indirectly connected with a perception, and no perception that is not more or less consciously connected with a movement. There is nothing in and of us that is fully removed from this base; even the images of fantasy, dreams, madness draw their material from it; our language is rooted in it."[18]

This claim is overly ambitious, but it is part of Buber's late attempt to think about sensation as a mutual endeavor involving us and material things.

How is this done? Buber first establishes a "circuit" [*Umkreis*] that passes between a human and a thing.[19] This circuit between the object and me involves more than just the two of us. It passes through things (light waves in air, vibrations in the earth) in a way that the I-You and forms of absolute presence do not; it is media dependent. In its most basic mode, sensuality is a physical link or connection between me and the thing I sense; in its more artistic or imaginal modes, sensuality is a transformation or completion of this physical relationship into an artwork, a dream, or some other form.

When we sense the material world, we are engaged in an asymmetrical relationship. Sensuality is a physical connection with a material object, but this connection is physical precisely because we are dealing with something (material) that does not depend on us. We are dependent on the material world for our existence, but the reverse is not the case unless one is in the middle of an Idealist fever.

I and x

And yet, we often think and act as if the material world is a mere extension of ourselves: Objects are just cybernetic limbs to be put on us unhappy gods, and matter is just lying there waiting, to be used. This tendency to view material reality as little more than "stuff" that we work with, valueless unless we grant it value, is the basis for the moral dictum that we should not treat people like things: Don't treat thinking beings like "stuff." But this tendency cannot be overcome as if it were a mere prejudice. A sensual circuit with a thing is very different from a language relationship with a person.[20] Knowing that someone views themselves as an "I" makes it easier for me to think of them as independent, as being something other than an extension of my needs. But things cannot say "I" and do not discursively assert their independence: They can't tell me to back off and leave them alone; they don't declare their own desires.

Because objects don't push back I can too easily assume that my perception exhausts them that outside of my seeing it or using one it, it's "just a thing." This habit of demeaning materiality leads to a bizarre inversion: the belief that the material world depends on us, and not the other way around. To counteract this error, Buber uses one of Kant's more obscure figures, the transcendental x, seen previously with the linden tree. The transcendental x is a way for us to think about material beings as independent of us: "I can only place [the object] in its independence by freeing it from the sense world, from its sensible representation. What then remains as it-self, emptied of all the properties that it has acquired in the meeting with me, in the sense world, may here be designated by a small x."[21] So when I first perceive something and then strip away my perceiving, what is left? Only an "x" remains.

Why the need for this "x"? The parallel with the "I," or the "self," is illustrative. The self cannot be identified by any property.[22] What makes you you, or me me, is intangible—it's not stored in a body part. So we use a placeholder and refer to this intangible quality with pronouns (*I, you*, or *she*). But these pronouns and placeholders tell us little more than nothing—hence the oddity that we use the same set of words (*I, you, she*) to refer to the most radically diverse singularities (different people).²³

Once the need for the "x" has been established, Buber places the perplexing and paradoxical aspects of the relationship onto it. A transcendental object is unthinkable, unimaginable, singular, and, in a strict sense, inimitable. It is not, for all that, unapproachable. This is the key to Buber's transformation of Kant: "Of x we *know* what Kant points out to us of the thing in-itself, namely, that it *is*. Kant would say: 'And nothing more,' but we . . . must add: 'and that existent *meets* us.' . . . For in all the world of the senses there is *no trait that does not stem from meetings*, that did not originate in the co-working of the x in the meeting."²⁴

This seemingly minor addition to Kant (that the "x" meets us halfway) is more significant than it might seem. By insisting that this object plays as much a role as we do in sensation, Buber marks a clear line between himself and the Idealists. All sensuality occurs neither in us nor in the world, but between us and the world. The one thing I can say about anything I perceive is that it participates in sensation.²⁵

It is a short distance from participation to movement. To clarify, sensuality is a space between the object and I where we both participate. Sensing is thus neither fully active nor passive on our part—and neither is it a Goldilocks mixture of the two—but rather a coworking between the thing and I, which Buber describes (and not without reason) as a movement. Any object you are aware of has done something to appear to you, even if it only bounced some light waves in your direction. Your sensory apparatus is constantly moving and whirring. Working together, an appearance is formed.

Both the "x" and the "I," when taken by themselves, are invisible and unsensed. Sensation, or perception, occurs in between the two and involves both as actors of a sort: "My perception is . . . a natural act in which 'I' and 'x' take part."²⁶ Perception is not a mere copy of the "x" (which is impossible), and neither is it an expression of myself. Instead, sensation is the place where the I and x form things between each other. If the relation of complete presence is called "I-You," the sensual relation to mute things is I-x.²⁷ If the dash between the I and the You is a meeting in which both participate, here, the dash between the two terms, or the circuit that connects them, is sensation. So we now have something like mutuality, spontaneity, and interdependence: the basic ingredients of a dialogue.²⁸ This coworking is made tangible with crafting, which is also a process of formation that occurs between the "I" and the unknown "x," with the difference being that crafting changes things and so leaves a trace in the world to be seen by others in turn.

Creation

Craft, unlike sensation and perception, overtly changes the world: It creates things. For Buber, it is an intensification and consolidation of the formative process and motions involved in perception. This is both why and how Buber revaluated his earlier negative notion of form. As Braiterman notes, Buber's change of heart is easy to miss in English translation. When he derides form in "Lesser Ury," he uses the German word *Form*, but when he later develops a more affirmative notion of form, he uses the word *Gestalt*. Why is *Gestalt* good, while *Form* is bad? Buber conceived *Form* as unmoving, hostile to dynamism, while *Gestalt* is part of a process.[29] The *Gestalt* that emerges at the end of a creative process not only contains traces of the dynamism that produced it but is also able to reenter the conflict between the formed and the formless to be transformed anew.

Once Buber developed a more appreciative view of form (as *Gestalt*), he was also able to develop a more materialist notion of creation. In early life Buber subscribed to something like an enthusiastic Nietzschean aesthetics, where form stands as a false imposition or constraining of vital forces. But by 1912, at the latest, Buber had developed a more sophisticated account of creation as a working together of the formative and the formless, rather than a war between form and motion. We see this in his deep affection for Michelangelo's famous *Slaves*, where unfinished torsos exhibit the tense relationship between rough stone and smooth carving.[30] Buber draws from these statues the lesson that creation is never one-and-done; it is a continual act.

This is further developed in "Man and His Image Work," where Buber discusses the decorative arts. Here, Buber foregrounds the material "stuff," or substratum, of art and craft as a *participant* in the process. This participation in creation mirrors the role of materiality in perception, albeit raised to a higher intensity. So, where perception can be viewed as a coworking between "I" and the "x," creation is a coworking between me and the material I am working with. And while here, my role in the process is more obvious, as I chisel, draw, or slice the material, the material's role is also more explicit, as its whorls, contours, impurities, or grain guide the process and the emerging form.

Of course, this all depends on what type of creation we are talking about. Buber's focus in "Image Work" is the decorative, but it can be expanded to other crafts. There are, however, types of creation excluded from his theory. We can roughly divide creative processes between those that impose form onto material and those that develop forms through an encounter with materials. Craft requires working with already existing material on which the process is dependent. This is why Buber thinks Genesis 1 is a bad model for thinking about creativity.[31] Both biblical creation and human creativity are concerned with the emergence of something new, but where biblical creation is autonomous—an autonomy expressed very forcefully by the ex nihilo interpretation—human creativity happens in a real place, using already existing things that push back and limit the process.[32] Where God develops form out of itself, or out of nothing, the human finds forms in relationships with matter.

Tools

Crafting relationships with matter is potentially dialogical in a manner analogous to sensation. Much as I and the x cowork in the production of sensation, both I and the material contribute to the formation of a sensual object. But the formation of a craft differs from the emergence of a sensation because it requires the transformation of the matter (or x). To craft, you likely *use* tools, but this doesn't stop them from participating in dialogue. Our relationships with them are literally instrumental, and yet intense dialogues routinely occur with them and through them.

All this despite the tiresome prohibition against treating others "like a thing." This admonition is made without giving any thought to how we actually treat things, and it assumes that we treat all things merely as objects to be *exhausted*, that the value of an object lies entirely in what it does for me and how it extends my power: all means, no ends. But this is false. In crafting, use and uselessness are combined. I use a glue gun to affix eyes to a pom-pom my son has just wound, and the result of these instrumental relations is useless—an end in itself, if anything is.

Tools help us appreciate the ambivalence of our relationships with mute things; we engage *and* use tools, relate to *and* through them. This ambivalence grows when we use tools to make arts and crafts, where sensuality is a matter of not only apprehension but also formation. If reciprocity lies at the base of sensation, how much more so for crafting? If mere seeing is relational, how much more so is kneading, cutting, or drawing?

Buber's discussion of tools occurs sporadically over his career but is given its greatest detail in "What Is Man?" (1938). Buber opens with Kant's famous question "What is Man?" and then goes through a series of philosophical anthropologies to determine which, if any, are capable of answering Kant's question.[33] Unsurprisingly, all are found lacking, even Kant's, because they focus on human activity and ability at the expense of human relationships.[34] And for Buber, relationships are the pivotal issue for philosophical anthropology: To understand human beings, you must understand human relationships.[35] In other words, it is not the human ability to use tools that interests Buber so much as the relationships that we form with them.

It is Heidegger, not Kant, who is the text's primary adversary.[36] Unfortunately, Buber's reading of Heidegger isn't great, boiling down to saying that "Heidegger's 'existence' is monological" and that Heidegger's fatal flaw is his inability to appreciate dialogue.[37] Perhaps this is so. For now, I focus exclusively on Heidegger as Buber conceived him and ignore the many fair responses that Heidegger, or a Heideggerian, would give.

As part of his critique, Buber claims Heidegger doesn't really understand tools and our relationship with them.[38] Heidegger's error is not that he begins with everyday tool use but rather that Heidegger has an inadequate concept of the "everyday." In Buber's reading, Heidegger's monological notion of existence bears fruit in a deficient philosophical anthropology. Heidegger's everyday is organized around use and practicality, which Buber rejects as an improper understanding of the quotidian: "The man who gazes without purpose on a tree is no less 'everyday' than the one who looks at a tree to learn which branch would make the best stick."[39] Even if they are speaking past each other, there is some appeal to Buber's position.

What is a better model for thing-relationships than Heidegger's tools? Buber claims that the "completion," or realization, of the relationship to things is found in "art."[40] Not the observation, enjoyment, or experience of art but the creative relationship, in making things, in craft. Why? Because the crafting relationship involves *both* instrumentality *and* reciprocity: "Art can only be understood in the connection of an essential with a technical relation."[41] Simply put, you can't make most art without a mechanical relationship, but the mechanical relationship must work in tandem with another form of relationship, one that is intimate and close to the "second person." It is this duality—*instrumentality in tandem with reciprocal intimacy*—that constitutes the "complete" thing-relation.

We are a long way away from any ethical connoisseurship or a respect for the tool's radical otherness. Tool dialogues—dialogues both with and through tools—most often occur while using them. It's when we use tools that they push back, giving us a tangible basis for dialogue. Peeling an apple or slicing a pepper where the knife catches the grain in the vegetable is a basic case where material, via the tool, directs us. Of course, the tool and the pepper are completely unaware of us as individuals, but it is a form of reciprocity, however minute.

Buber draws this affection for tools from Hasidic sources.[42] He reads them as he reads most religious and cultural objects: not as "rational" but imaginal, meaning knowledge "communicable only in images, not in concepts."[43] What is the image he derives from these sources? The idea is that life, or at least domestic life, is a series of enclosures, "a natural circle of things" that we are to cultivate.[44] Why? For the sake of many small encounters, including "the materials [*Naturstoffe*] we shape, the tools we use." There is a moral component to these encounters: "If we think only in terms of momentary purposes, without developing a genuine relationship to the beings and things in whose life we ought to take part, as they in ours, then we shall ourselves be debarred from true, fulfilled existence."[45] Tools and materials provide opportunities for relationships, and if we ignore this, our lives are impoverished.

What interests me is not so much the moral push to encounter things but the nature of the encounters: "The materials we shape, the tools we use, they all contain a mysterious spiritual substance [*Seelensubstanz*] which depends on us for helping it toward its pure form [*Gestalt*], its perfection [*Vollendung*]."[46] What exactly is meant here by perfection, or completion, of form is debatable, but this neo-Hasidic process, where we encounter spirit in the stuff of the world and then help or coax it into becoming what it is, is homologous to Buber's (admittedly less dramatic) account of crafting, where forms emerge from an encounter with tools and materials.[47]

So, we've sketched a series of relationships that all operate in a similar manner: perception, tool use, and crafting. Buber claims these relationships all exhibit a degree of mutuality and dismisses interpretations where perception, tool use, or art are explained as the imposition of a form by a sovereign creator onto plastic matter. Instead, we have various forms of coworking between us and the material world, in each case mediated differently, but in each case capable of reciprocation and, thus, dialogue. At a minimum, Buber is telling a story about these three material relationships with the intention of explaining his bold claim that we can dialogue with anything we are aware of.[48] For all of these relationship models, reciprocity, however thin, is possible. Buber is also grounding dialogue in our most basic material relationships: Dialogue is not given from on high but is rather a potential of all relationships.

But dialogue is not a matter of mere reciprocity, even if it often takes the form of passing something back and forth. Dialogue also requires intimacy and engagement, and these we find illustrated with even greater clarity in the decorative arts.

Decoration

Craft differs from sensation because it usually involves intention toward, and intimacy with, a thing, which Buber compares to a love relationship. A craftsperson is not content to just look at a thing; they want to be directed toward it and realize the engagement in a manner that leaves a trace or changes something. Hence, Buber's insistence (elliptically mocked by Adorno) that we can overcome our alienation from things in an immediate manner, a desire that underpins the crafting relationship (and not the Idealist-industrial-creator relationship where form is imposed).[49] This type of craft is a process of formation that is not an imposition of a form from on high or a copying of the object's form (because the "x" does not have a form to copy) but an extrapolation, coaxing, or development of a form between the material and the person, the "I" and the "x."[50] Craft is a deepening, or intensification, of this mutuality that is found in sensation, issuing in transformed sensuality. As Klee famously wrote, "Art does not reproduce the visible, rather it *makes* visible," and Buber claims something similar.[51]

Decoration is a form of craft that manipulates matter almost entirely for sensual purposes. Unlike high art, decoration is generally unconcerned with concepts and art history; it is certainly part of the latter, but rarely does it seek to critique, say, the role of galleries or the function of the observer. When the decorative arts go to art history, they generally do so to brazenly steal from it, as is proper. Decoration is part of aesthetics in the old sense of the term: It is concerned with sculpting sensuality, sometimes with a specific effect in mind (as when we decorate a room to create a cozy atmosphere), sometimes as an intensification of something already existing (sewing patches on a leather jacket, arranging vegetables on the kitchen counter to show them off).

Buber's most philosophically developed treatment of craft occurs in "Distance and Relation" (1950), where a boy etches a curved line on an ax. There are two tools in this story: a stone ax and a sharper stone used to trace a line on it. That the story is tool-centric is not incidental—a tool is an ideal object for decoration because it has been plucked out of "nature" and set at a distance from us. Unlike a random stone, it has been given an identity of some sort. Once a tool is distanced, it has a degree of autonomy; it remains at a distance even when unused—which is why we store tools—and so has a "place in a world."[52] A stone ax may not have a name, but it has been individuated, identified as a singular thing, which makes it easier to approach it as an "x."

But the distanced object only provides the situation. After it has been distanced, "something new and essentially different can enter the situation." Meaning, we can start to talk about relationships. And the first relationship Buber discusses is decoration.[53]

In Buber's story, it occurs to someone to "scratch a curved line in his axe with the aid of a sharper stone. This is a picture of something and of nothing; it may be a sign, but even its author knows not of what."[54] Let us break down this vignette into its parts. First, consider the thing itself. Imagine a decorative whorl of some sort, purposeless and intense, drawn with a gesture. The gesture results in an image of "something and of nothing" because it's neither mimesis nor expression, "neither the impression of natural objectivity nor the expression of spiritual subjectivity."[55] The form—the curved line—is drawn from withing the interaction between the human and the ax; it's not an attempt to draw some other object. But neither is it nothing, any more than a grotesque or a flourish in a manuscript is nothing. It's a thing, a new thing, which emerges from the relationship.

The relationship between the human and thing "is the work and witness of the relation between the *substantia humana* and the *substantia rerum*, it is the realm of the 'in between' which has *become* a form."[56] This in-between, this neither subjective nor objective place between the boy and the ax, is the space of a dynamic back-and-forth relationship where forms are developed. We have crossed the border from dynamism into dialogue, even if it is a dialogue between two "substances," of which only one is a person. The form of the ax is completed by this trace on the handle. Under this model, the completed craft is "the *sediment* of man's relation to things."[57] This is not a metaphor. The ax handle is impressed with a real mark left by the relationship.

Finally, why is the line, this "something and nothing," curved? One can easily make too much of a detail, but I suggest that the curve is a typical result of the coworking between the person decorating and the thing being decorated. Rather than imposing a line on the ax handle, like a stamp on metal, the boy finds a nascent in the stone and develops it—the form is developed from an element found submerged in the undecorated handle. Here, I am adding a story on top of a story, but not without any basis. Gombrich notes that, especially in decorative art and craft, it is common to take a flourish found in material and develop it into a figure: driving, or pushing, figures out of the flourish's kinetic potential.[58] A whorl in the stone or wood is extrapolated on, or extended, and so a form is developed. There is a lovely illustration of this in Klee's journals: "In the restaurant run by my uncle, the fattest man in Switzerland, were tables topped with polished marble slabs, whose surface displayed a maze of petrified layers. In this labyrinth of lines one could pick out human grotesques and capture them with a pencil. I was fascinated with this pastime; my bent for the bizarre announced itself."[59]

We are far removed from the ancient frame that Buber postulates but there is a symmetry between these two stories.[60] The little Klee "picks out" forms hidden in the marble table and captures them with a pencil, forming a grotesque out of the marble's natural texture. This is akin to "scratching" a figure into an ax. Both are dynamic meetings that "drive" the crafting of images, a process where both the person and the seemingly formless material play a role. In both, the young artist or the boy with his ax develops shapes out of their sensual relationships; they are skilled perceivers, sensual savants.

For Buber, matter is full of specific potencies, or possible forms that cowork in the crafting of figures. Matter "meets" us through these potencies—its swirls, lines, textures, and other seemingly germinal forms—much as we meet it through sensation and movement. In this sense, matter is infinite, rather than merely indefinite. Seeing these textures as germinal movements helps us understand one way an image can form between a human and "material."

There are many such instances of drawing forms out of the seemingly random whorls in stone, my favorite being pictorial stones, a form of painting most popular in the seventeenth century, where artists would find figures in marble or agate and develop them with paint.[61] Baltrušaitis notes these stones "differ from painted pictures because of the depth of their penetration. They do not lie on the surface, like the figures executed by an artist. They penetrate the entire depth of the stone."[62] These images "spring from" their agate or jasper base: The stone guides the craftsperson, who in turn brings a catalog of images to contribute to the process.[63]

Similarly, the images Klee develops are derived not from general concepts but out of a relation to matter itself. It is a dialogue with something that has been distanced (the manufactured tabletop). No, the stone does not say "I"; its singularity cannot be derived in any way from its consciousness or my ability to talk to it. Here, the reciprocity and spontaneity are grounded in sensuality and movement, and pencil markings, not speech, actualize the encounter, however transitory. But it is, for all that, a form of dialogue.

Manufactured Homes

Most of our material engagement is far more mundane, more domestic than the instances given by Buber and Klee. The vast majority of my engagement with crafts and tools occurs in my home, playing with my children, fixing things, playing music, and, of course, cooking. The temporality of thing engagement is impossible to delineate in advance—it very much depends on the thing. A red pepper opens up to a knife immediately, but the knife may take years to develop a relationship with, if it happens at all (and it rarely does).

As always, the fact that we have some kind of relationship with a thing does not in any way mean that it is dialogical, let alone "good." Many relationships are abstract and alienated, and many dialogues are painful or cruel. Buber's model of sensation, his interpretation of tool use, and his philosophy of art all show ways it is possible to dialogue with material things. And this, in turn, shows how it is possible to say that the limits of dialogue are the limits of awareness. But none of these in and of themselves "create" dialogue; they merely allow it. Cultivating these interactions into dialogues requires a good deal more work and attention, and it sometimes seems that the entire world militates against this.

Nowhere is it harder for me to determine whether a relationship is dialogical or merely comforting than with manufactured objects. It's easier to do so with repairing and maintaining. When I repair a wall, I am trying to maintain a space while also working with it in a manner that sometimes seems reciprocal, if hostile. The tools I use vacillate between being media through which I engage material, and being themselves a kind of conversation partner. With cooking, it is easier to dialogue. With arts, crafts, and decoration, it is easier still. Immersed in material, I can work with it to find and create things. And there is something of a circle here. With decoration, the attempt to maintain a space that encourages dialogue (through its warmth or richness) can easily veer into becoming a dialogue itself. And so on until we die.

CONCLUSION
Death and Dialogue

My father died over the course of writing this book, and it was not an easy death. It was long and painful and involved stretching knifelike moments into weeks. My father was a stubborn tank of a man; the same labor that poisoned him made him strong, and so he approached death unevenly. Parts of him died before others refused to quit, and in the last week or so, he was unable to speak.

People who die as he did need to be cared for long after it's clear there is no chance for recovery. It was hard to know when the line was crossed, but once we moved him from the home to the hospice, we knew it was irreversible. My father, like many others, wanted to die in a home. Hospitals are horrible places, all edges and bright lights and bitterness; they are cold. The hospice was initially viewed as a compromise: Someone would be there to help clean his shit and give him injections; not as good as a home, but better than a hospital.

The reality was stranger. The hospice, Matthew's House (as it is called) was a third thing. Homelike without being a home—sometimes more homelike than our actual home. It was staffed by people I'd not met before, people who feel called to help others die. There were, broadly speaking, two types of these people: The normal people, the volunteers, helped to support us so we could (in the words of a friend) help my father through the final veil. The others, nurses willing to work for far less than they would be paid at a hospital, helped coax him along, removing obstacles and pain where they could. The first group seemed motivated by something like charity or kindness; the latter (and this is only from conversation, not study) seemed motivated by the meaning of death.

My father was a difficult and lovely man, and as it were, he closed out the bar. We arrived to a full house, and even after every single person there had died, he kept going. He was tough. For the last week or so, every day we were told, "This is it, there is no chance he keeps going." He was on enough painkillers to kill a normal person twice over. The doctor walked into the room, looked at him refusing to die, and threw up her hands. She said one word, "How?" and walked out. The same man who refused to speak directly for fear of cliché (or, as he called it, "boilerplate") ended his life with the same headstrong strangeness.

What does this have to do with dialogue? A few things. First, my father's labyrinthine way of speaking was infamous. It was routinely suggested that he study English as a second language. Growing up in an immigrant home does not explain it. He was circuitous to the point that another doctor resisted approving him for assisted suicide because the doctor read his rambling refusal to touch on a subject directly as mental incapacitation.

All of us, his children, had received a strange training in language and deciphering. We all learned how to speak his idiosyncratic language and, more importantly, interpret a man who steadfastly refused to say the same thing twice. We became good at interpreting strange speech, experts at interpreting him.

The second thing is that slow death is strange death. In the end, his heart and lungs were strong and refused to stop, even though it appeared all conscious thought, and certainly all conscious expression, had departed. Near the end, he was dispersed; it was hard to locate his life—where was it? In the heart, which kept a steady rhythm, in the mind, which no longer spoke, in the hands, which moved in an erratic manner, or in his face, which twitched and seemed to smile and frown?

The question—how do you dialogue with something that cannot speak?—took on urgency. My siblings and I basically lived in Matthew's House. At first, for a month, there was a great deal of talking. My father tried to purchase his own urn on Amazon because he thought he would get a better deal than we would. After much debate, he relented and allowed a friend to make him one. He also read about a company that offered a service: They would train an AI to speak like the departed, or departing, so that you could converse with them after they were gone. I have no doubt this wouldn't have worked: My father's speech was too odd, the technology was too undeveloped, and the uncanny valley of death would be cruelly obvious. But, in time, something like this will be possible, if it isn't already. My father thought forcing me to listen to him beyond the grave was funny. I thought it was horrifying, but I didn't know why.

Now I do because I see how talk can obscure dialogue by giving it an artificial stability. This means that when it really matters, when we are trying to do the work of death and speak to a speechless and dispersed person, we are unprepared. Or, rather, worse than unprepared—we have been actively untrained, damaged, even, by false talk.

What do I mean by this maudlin train of thought? Is this nonsense that has been given extra weight by a morbid story? Perhaps it is, but I don't think so. I suggest, and it's only a suggestion, that the speech engines teach us literally less than nothing. Obscuring the limit of the human, and so itself, and so us in turn, all because of our lazy desire to have signals presented as symbols, a refusal to dialogue without language.

When speech disappeared, we were left with bodies. Bodies, gross bodies, trying to pass feelings and messages back and forth between them. My father, a warped and rarely silent river of symbols, at the edge of his life was reduced to signals—and we were reduced to hoping we weren't merely projecting onto his moving face. Who knows, maybe we were. Projection is always a problem with dialogue, and it only increases when you have no speech, a problem silent beings force us to face, to be trained in, in a way that seemingly speaking machines do not.

Sitting there, trying to send out feelings and read desires with my father—hoping when we told him of love, that the twitch of his lips was a recognition, that the movement of an eyebrow was him saying something to us: I hear you, I love you, I remember that too—this was as fragile as a dialogue with a cat, as messy as one with a baby, diffused over our plantlike surfaces. And I messed it up, at least once, by being impatient with the stubborn stupidity of our signals. His angry wince in response might have been from some unseen cancer pain, but I read it as a reproach: getting upset that I was trying to hurry him. This is how it is when you are reading every glimmer as a signal; it's easy to make mistakes. But I pulled from years of speaking with unspeaking beings to guide me. And mostly, it worked.

Am I saying that dialogue with unspeaking tools and organisms prepared me for this? Yes, I am saying that. And am I saying that setting up a chatbot that would mimic the dead may well damage people's ability to do this? I am saying that as well.

With babies and the dying, dialogue without speaking becomes human. Surrounding us, shared by animals, probably plants, possibly things, dialogue is pre- and postlinguistic—it encloses language. Speaking is a wondrous instance of dialogue, but laying kisses on flickering eyes and trying to read the unreadable is what we begin and end with.

NOTES

Introduction

1. For a famous and artful articulation of the grid world, see fellow Viennese weirdo Ludwig Wittgenstein:

> 1. The world is all that is the case.
>
> 1.1 The world is the totality of facts, not of things.
>
> 1.11 The world is determined by the facts, and by their being all the facts.
>
> 1.12 For the totality of facts determines what is the case, and also whatever is not the case.
>
> 1.13 The facts in logical space are the world.

Ludwig Wittgenstein, *Tractatus Logico-Philosophicus*, trans. Michael Beaney (Oxford University Press, 2023), 1.

2. What to call these things creates problems. The word *thing* can be alienating, especially because of the often-repeated rule to "not treat people like things." Indeed, all of the words to refer to nonhumans in a generic manner (*thing, being, object, entity, creature*) carry baggage. I largely reject and ignore this baggage and use these words rather interchangeably when not explicitly using technical phenomenological terms—but I try to avoid *thing* because of its negative associations (which I don't share) and *object*, except when describing an intentional relationship or grammatical form.

3. The grammatical person, or stance, runs throughout Buber's work, whether through pronouns (in *I and Thou*), theological positions (*Emunah* and *Pistis* in *Two Types of Faith*), or presence versus experience.

4. Hence the odd relationship between dialogue and feeling. I can have a strong relationship without strong feelings, and strong feelings without a strong relationship. This is something of a problem when we are trained to expect feelings and relationships to operate in parallel.

5. There are many ways of being directed, or paying attention, but grammatically speaking, dialogue is almost entirely in the second person. Stephen Darwell has made a career out of Buber's grammatical insight. It is, of course, more than possible that he arrived at it without Buber, but the near exclusion of Buber from his citations is still surprising.

6. "Talking-to" is perhaps best seen as a shorthand for the intentional stance one takes in dialogue; once the dialogue gets going, it is better described as talking-with. However, as this book deals almost exclusively with beings whose intentional stance is mysterious to us, I use *talking-to* so as to avoid unnecessary presumptions about our dialogue partners.

7. Plato, *Phaedrus*, trans. A. Nehamas and P. Woodruff (Hackett, 1995), 231a.

8. This is why dialogue is more a phenomenological concern than an ontological one.

9. It is here—with the notion of a seductive writer, or "indirect communication"—that Buber's work most closely emulates Kierkegaard's. As he writes in *Dialogue*, "What I am here concerned with cannot be conveyed in *ideas* to a reader. But we may represent it by

examples—provided that, where the matter is important, we do not eschew taking examples from the inmost recesses of the personal life." Martin Buber, *Between Man and Man*, Routledge Classics (Routledge, 2002), 6; Søren Kierkegaard, *Concluding Unscientific Postscript to the Philosophical Crumbs*, trans. Alastair Hannay, Cambridge Texts in the History of Philosophy (Cambridge University Press, 2009), 252, 77; Kierkegaard, *The Point of View*, trans. H. V. Hong and E. H. Hong (Princeton University Press, 1998), 25–51.

10. Charles S. Peirce, *Essential Peirce* (Indiana University Press, 1992, 1998), 227.

11. I confine myself mostly to Buber's examples, with the addition of several I am familiar with. Why examples? Who cares about objects that are supposed to be little more than a place to "test" what really matters—our ideas? Because dialogues are a type of encounter, so—as much as I might wish otherwise—examples are what we have to "point" to, to test out our notions. This test always involves a degree of inhabiting the example ourselves. As we will be talking-about talking-to, this requires a degree of acting on our part: to inhabit the roles, if only in imagination, in order to think about them.

12. This transposition reflects a significant contribution from Jewish philosophy—and philosophy in general—whenever its concepts are extraphilosophical. I use *Jewish philosophy* in Zev-Harvey's capacious manner, to mean "any philosophy that is created in some meaningful way against the background of Jewish life or culture, just as French philosophy is any philosophy created in a meaningful way against that of French life." Warren Zev Harvey, "Jewish Philosophy for the Twenty-First Century: Personal Reflections," in *Jewish Philosophy Tomorrow: Post-Messianic and Post-Lachrymose*, ed. Hava Tirosh-Samuelson and Aaron W. Hughes (Brill, 2014).

13. I would note that the "in-between," or the much-vaunted "ontology of the in-between," is an absolute red herring, one I wasted much of my PhD fishing for. Buber simply does not have an ontology of the in-between as the in-between is (for him) something more like a transcendental condition for dialogue than a way to understand "being." Martin Buber, *Philosophical Interrogations: Interrogations of Martin Buber, John Wild, Jean Wahl, Brand Blanshard, Paul Weiss, Charles Hartshorne, Paul Tillich*, ed. Sydney Chester Rome and Beatrice K. Rome (Holt, 1964), 23, 27; Michael Theunissen, *The Other: Studies in the Social Ontology of Husserl, Heidegger, Sartre, and Buber* (MIT Press, 1984), 257. For a different stance on Buber's ontological predilections, see Herskowitz. Where I depart from Herskowitz's (excellent) reading is that I don't think Buber is seriously engaged in an ontological project—he is more interested in form and relation than being. Even though he constantly refers to "being," as Herskowitz notes, Buber seriously misconstrues Heidegger's project and also misconstrues ontology as it would come to be known in the twentieth century. Buber does not have much to say about the ontological difference. Daniel Herskowitz, *Heidegger and His Jewish Reception* (Cambridge University Press, 2020), 128–34. For a treatment of the in-between and its relationship to Buber's late dialogical work, see Wolfson: "In his dialogical stage Buber claimed that unity is realized—continuously and never absolutely—in the 'Between,' i.e., in the meeting of two beings who nevertheless remain distinct." The in-between has an ontological "side" but is neither grounded there nor even constituted there. As Wolfson illustrates, the between is *both* like a cause and an effect of actual beings, and so is not ontological in a Heideggerian or Aristotelian sense. I follow Wolfson's periodization of Buber's project throughout this book. Elliot R. Wolfson, "The Problem of Unity in the Thought of Martin Buber," *Journal of the History of Philosophy* 27, no. 3 (1989): 424.

14. Here, I largely follow Kavka, who writes, "My goal is to develop a reconstruction of Buber that saves him from himself, and contributes to saving the modern Jewish thought

canon from becoming irrelevant as a result of its problems." Why do this? Why force Buber's philosophy to contort in ways he did not intend? Kavka answers, "First, Jewish philosophy will simply become bad philosophy; Buber, for example, will become someone of note either simply for his ethnicity or because he influenced people susceptible to bad or unclear arguments. Second, the longer it remains undecided how to read Buber—or how to improve him—the easier it will be to reduce all of Buber to mere rhetoric." Martin Kavka, "Verification (Bewährung) in Martin Buber" [in English], *Journal of Jewish Thought and Philosophy* 20, no. 1 (2012): 76. I disagree with Kavka about Buber being transcendental. Yes, supralogical must be *expressed* logically, which means using the language of transcendence, but, as the rewriting of the lectures in *On Judaism* shows, the mature Buber is committed to neither immanence nor transcendence as a principle. Finally, I follow Kavka in bringing Buber's work into contact with pragmaticism, but I choose Peirce over James.

15. Horwitz's book provides an excellent guide to Buber's early and middle thought on presence. Wolfson articulates the late model pithily: It is through the presence of Thou that the present comes to be. For Buber, the present exists only insofar as there is relationship, encounter. "Only as the You becomes present does presence come into being. The presentness of presence is that which cannot be re-presented." Rivka Horwitz and Martin Buber, *Buber's Way to "I and Thou": The Development of Martin Buber's Thought and His "Religion as Presence" Lectures*, 1st American ed. (Jewish Publication Society, 1988); Wolfson, "The Problem of Unity in the Thought of Martin Buber."

16. For the young Buber, the goal of the religious person is to realize god in the world (through a form of self-negating unification). This type of realization ceased to be the goal of religious life for Buber around the time he published *I and Thou* (1923), but it remained as a way of making encounters real or bringing their fruits into the world. Horwitz and Buber, *Buber's Way to "I and Thou."*

17. Intuition pumps are thought experiments designed to introduce and elucidate concepts and arguments by way of intuitions. According to Dennett: "Little stories designed to provoke a heartfelt, table-thumping intuition—'Yes, of course, it has to be so!'—about whatever thesis is being defended. I have called these intuition pumps. . . . Intuition pumps have been a dominant force in philosophy for centuries. They are the philosophers' version of Aesop's fables, which have been recognized as wonderful thinking tools since before there were philosophers." D. C. Dennett, *Intuition Pumps and Other Tools for Thinking* (Norton, 2013), 5.

18. A note on the sources: Although I use *I and Thou* throughout this book to elucidate the notion of dialogue, *I and Thou* is not primarily concerned with dialogue but rather with absolute presence. Martin Buber, *I and Thou*, trans. Walter Arnold Kaufmann (Scribner, 1970), 61.

19. Buber, *Philosophical Interrogations*, 20.

20. Martin Buber, ed., "Dialogue," in *Between Man and Man* (Routledge, 2002), 5.

21. My understanding of the importance of the mundane for Buber owes a great deal to discussion with Gregory Kaplan.

22. As Buber notes, "Just as the most eager speaking at one another does not make a conversation (this is most clearly shown in that curious sport, aptly termed discussion [*Diskussion*], that is, 'breaking apart,' which is indulged in by men who are to some extent gifted with the ability to think)." Buber, "Dialogue," 3.

23. Buber, "Dialogue," 3.

24. Buber, "Dialogue," 43.

25. Habermas, who is in turn citing *I and Thou*.

> The feature that sets human beings apart from animals is not self-reflection in the sense of turning a reiterated subject–object or I–It relationship upon oneself. Our lives are instead performed in the triadic communicative relationship between a first and a second person while communicating about objects in the world. The phenomenon of self-consciousness is derived from dialogue: "The person becomes conscious of himself as sharing in being, as co-existing." [Buber] In advance of any explicit self-reflection, the subject is caught up in an interpersonal relationship and first becomes aware of herself performatively by adopting the perspective of the other towards herself.

As useful as Habermas can be for clarifying abstruse ideas, here (as elsewhere), this is done at the cost of detail. Habermas does not seem to see any difference between language and dialogue—indeed, where he writes *dialogue*, I would suggest reading *language* or *talking*. Jürgen Habermas, "A Philosophy of Dialogue," in *Dialogue as a Trans-Disciplinary Concept*, ed. Paul Mendes-Flohr, Martin Buber's Philosophy of Dialogue and Its Contemporary Reception (De Gruyter, 2015).

26. George Carlin, *Back in Town* (Atlantic, 1996), sound recording, 1 sound disc: digital; 4 3/4 in., 92728-2 Atlantic.

27. Buber, "Dialogue," 12.

28. Wolfe reminds us that "the distinction between language and nonlanguage is itself made within language," so these types are drawn from within language or, less poetically, by language users. This does not require us to view these types as reductive or to trap nonhumans in language "because the outside is the outside of the inside, the differential or 'incalculable' structure of alterity is preserved." Wolfe's work is driven in part by a concern for the ethical treatment of animals, and thus "alterity" is a ground for good behavior—a position I cannot share. Cary Wolfe, *Animal Rites: American Culture, the Discourse of Species, and Posthumanist Theory* (University of Chicago Press, 2008), 205. Further, this leads to a dismissal (in the tradition of Deleuze) of any asymmetrical power relationships between humans and animals (the pet, the trained animal) as poisoned from the start, as "Oedipal and narcissistic." I would rather say that relations of imbalance, or even open conflict, make it harder to not project but do not therefore render the relationship moot. The parent-child relationship and the teacher-student relationship, among others, are complicated and open to abuse, but they are not always narcissistic. Where I find myself more amenable to Wolfe is his Lyotard-inspired work on animals and language, which preserves animal difference without subjugating nonhumans to the kingdom of words. G. Deleuze and F. Guattari, *A Thousand Plateaus: Capitalism and Schizophrenia* (Athlone Press, 1988), 4.

29. I explore the three spheres from an anthropological perspective, with an emphasis on relation to objects, in Dustin Atlas, "How to Do Things with Things: Craft at the Edge of Buber's Philosophical Anthropology" (in English), *IMAGES* 12, no. 1 (2019): 137. Buber, *I and Thou*, 56, 149.

30. This is unfortunate because I read Buber as advocating for the creation and maintenance of spheres, rather than living in the "grid world" of external relations. His use of the term *spheres* here confuses the little places and worlds we create, and Buber's models for relation.

31. Buber added,

> Animals are not twofold, like man: the twofoldness of the basic words I-You and I-It is alien to them although they can both turn toward another being and contemplate

objects. We may say that in them twofoldness is latent. In the perspective of our You-saying to animals, we may call this sphere the *threshold of mutuality*. It is altogether different with those realms of nature which lack the spontaneity that we share with animals. It is part of our concept of the plant that it cannot react to our actions upon it, that it cannot "reply." Yet this does not mean that we meet with no reciprocity at all in this sphere.... What matters in this sphere is that we should do justice with an open mind to the actuality that opens up before us. This huge sphere that reaches from the stones to the stars *I should like to designate as the prethreshold, meaning the step that comes before the threshold."*

The threshold does a lot of work here, but the salient fact seems to be that it is *neither entirely within nor without language*. Bakhtin's work on Dostoevsky is helpful for fleshing out what a threshold *is* (a place where things change, where character is revealed, and so on); it is certainly more helpful than the image of a sphere. Buber, *I and Thou*, 173. Mikhail Bakhtin, *Problems of Dostoevsky's Poetics*, trans. C. Emerson (University of Minnesota Press, 1984).

32. Buber, *I and Thou*, 59.

33. Buber, *Between Man and Man*, 115 (emphasis added).

34. Andrea Dworkin, *Right-Wing Women: The Politics of Domesticated Females* (Women's Press, 1983), 143.

35. Laura Levitt, *Jews and Feminism: The Ambivalent Search for Home* (Routledge, 1997).

1. Homes

1. You cannot force a dialogue, but you can prepare for it. Dialogues take many forms: Some are self-focused, such as opening ourselves up to the world or being patient, and others are outward, such as trying to *facilitate* dialogue by giving it a place and bringing potential partners together.

2. See Tronto and her analyses of communities of care. As she notes, "caring about, and taking care of, are the duties of the powerful. Care-giving and care-receiving [the domestic] are left to the less powerful." Tronto's excellent work suffers from the same problem that most ethical work does: the desire to see the highest (caring for one another) in the lowest (things appear to us *as* things we care about). The move from "caring about" to "caring for" is ultimately papered over. See, for instance, her section on "Elements of an Ethic of Care," which begins (correctly, I think) with "Attentiveness." But the gap between appearing and attentiveness remains. Things appear when I notice things I care about, or give a shit about, maybe because I want them or am afraid of them. I attend to things by focusing on them, and this shift from "passive" appearance to "active" attending is left hanging, like an assumed force of nature (here, buried in the sentiments). J. C. Tronto, *Moral Boundaries: A Political Argument for an Ethic of Care* (Routledge, 1993), 58, 59, 127.

3. M. Thalos, *Without Hierarchies: The Scale Freedom of the Universe* (Oxford University Press, 2013); Sarah Imhoff, "Homemaking in Palestine: Jessie Sampter, Religion, and Relation," in *At Home and Abroad*, ed. Hurd Elizabeth Shakman and Sullivan Winnifred Fallers (Columbia University Press, 2021).

4. This is one of the moral boundaries noted by Tronto: The ethical is placed in the house, and the political outside of it. This division holds even if one rejects Tronto's notion of the political (as a dispute over resource and order), which is part of Tronto's commitment to a liberal tradition (which arguably depends on this distinction). It is true that the

"philosophical tradition or political theory" does not attend to questions of "natality, mortality, and the needs of humans," provided one does not allow for any "religious" philosophy, including theopolitics and political theology, to say nothing of philosophy informed by materialism or psychoanalysis. Tronto, *Moral Boundaries*, 6, 10.

5. Hannah Arendt, *The Human Condition*, 2nd ed., trans. M. Canovan (University of Chicago Press, 2013), 24.

6. Arendt, *The Human Condition*, 38.

7. Note that this echoes Mendelssohn's theopolitics, but in *Jerusalem*, the social lies not between the house and the agora but between the church and the state. Moses Mendelssohn, *Jerusalem: Or on Religious Power and Judaism*, trans. Allan Arkush (Brandeis University Press, 1983).

8. Arendt, *The Human Condition*, 38, 59.

9. Here, as elsewhere, Arendt is beholden to Aristotle's *Politics*. Arendt, *The Human Condition*; Aristotle, *Politics: A New Translation*, trans. C. D. C. Reeve (Hackett, 2017), sec. 1259a.

10. Christopher Long, "A Fissure in the Distinction: Hannah Arendt, the Family and the Public/Private Dichotomy," *Philosophy & Social Criticism* 24, no. 5 (1998): 85–104.

11. Aristotle, *Politics*, 59a, 1252a.

12. Michael McKeon, *The Secret History of Domesticity: Public, Private, and the Division of Knowledge* (Johns Hopkins University Press, 2006), xvii.

13. McKeon, *The Secret History of Domesticity*, xix (emphasis added).

14. Eva Mroczek, "Without Torah or Scripture: Biblical Absence and the History of Revelation," *Hebrew Studies* 61 (2020): 97–110. Note that the mystical space is always complicated by a dialectical relationship with its own outside, and we should thus be cautious about applying this concern to this book. Wolfson's work on space and its creation is extensive, but of particular interest for this book is how enclosure is gendered. See, for instance, Elliot R. Wolfson, *Circle in the Square: Studies in the Use of Gender in Kabbalistic Symbolism* (State University of New York Press, 1995), chap. 4.

15. J. D. Levenson, *Creation and the Persistence of Evil: The Jewish Drama of Divine Omnipotence* (Princeton University Press, 1994). The first word in the Torah (*Bereshit*) begins with the second Hebrew letter (*Bet*), which sounds like the word for *house* (*Bayit*, often shortened to *Bat*).

16. Dworkin, *Right-Wing Women*, 143.

17. I thus follow Levitt, embracing neither the liberal household with its Attic heritage nor the traditional Jewish home. Levitt's project is multifaceted, and many of its issues—such as identity—are not germane to this book. Levitt, *Jews and Feminism*, 16.

18. Ultimately, the "liberal state has no compelling interest in what goes on within a man's home . . . making it difficult for those of us whose bodies have been violated at home to seek justice." Levitt, *Jews and Feminism*, 18, 19.

19. Levitt, *Jews and Feminism*, 94.

20. Charlotte Fonrobert, *Menstrual Purity: Rabbinic and Christian Reconstructions of Biblical Gender* (Stanford University Press, 2002), 58, 59. Bekhorot 45a, https://www.sefaria.org/Bekhorot.45a.19?lang=bi&with=all&lang2=en.

21. Fonrobert, *Menstrual Purity*, 65.

22. The chapter "Domesticity" in *Spinning Fantasies* is especially illuminating. Peskowitz notes how the Mishnah and the Talmud propose a world that strips the "woman of valour" of her power and make arrangements such that all female property and earnings are, in theory,

handed over to the male "head" of the house. M. B. Peskowitz, *Spinning Fantasies: Rabbis, Gender, and History* (University of California Press, 2023), 95–99. M. Lehman, *Bringing Down the Temple House: Engendering Tractate Yoma* (Brandeis University Press, 2022), 3.

23. I was given this insight by Meirav Jones.

24. Simply put, the home is constituted by "silent listening" to the father, which is the "ground" the home sits on. This domination, however, is tempered by the meal, in which the equality of the beginning is repeated/returned, establishing a space of mutual participation. Franz Rosenzweig, *The Star of Redemption*, trans. Barbara E. Galli, Modern Jewish Philosophy and Religion. Translations and Critical Studies (University of Wisconsin Press, 2005), 335; Andrea Dara Cooper, *Gendering Modern Jewish Thought* (Indiana University Press, 2021).

25. "The world in which reason becomes more and more self conscious is not habitable. It is hard and cold, like those supply depots where merchandise which cannot satisfy is piled up . . . it is impersonal, like factory hangars and industrial cities . . . true with the truth of calculations. . . . This is spirit in all its masculine essence. It lives outdoors . . . in a world that offers it no inner refuge, in which it is disorientated, solitary and wandering . . . alienated by the products it had helped to create." Emmanuel Levinas, *Difficult Freedom: Essays on Judaism*, Johns Hopkins Jewish Studies (Johns Hopkins University Press, 1990), 32.

26. As Katz has shown, Levinas's views on the feminine are modulated over the course of his life, and as he ages, he seeks the ethical in the feminine. Claire Katz, *Levinas, Judaism, and the Feminine: The Silent Footsteps of Rebecca* (Indiana University Press, 2003), 3. Here, we can see Levinas respond to Heidegger: It's not the house that matters, so much as the woman who lives there. With friends like these. Levinas, *Difficult Freedom*, 32.

27. Maria Carson, "The Emotional Heschel" (PhD diss., Syracuse University, 2021), 87, 123. https://surface.syr.edu/etd/1422/.

28. There are traces of this already in Abraham Heschel's *Sabbath*, but these are made far more concrete in Susannah Heschel's introduction appended in 2005. Abraham Heschel, *The Sabbath*, (Farrar, Straus and Giroux, 2005), vii, xi, 19, 30.

29. Even in the most liberal of arrangements, protection is assumed by the state, but if it is lacking, little is done. This is rendered more egregious by the fact that women and children are expected to give up their liberty for the sake of this protection. Levitt, *Jews and Feminism*, 18–19. When we veer "right," things get even worse. Dworkin writes, "Women are brought up to maintain a husband's home and to believe that women without men are homeless. Women have a deep fear of being homeless—at the mercy of the elements and of strange men. The Right claims to protect the home and the woman's place in it." Dworkin, *Right-Wing Women*, 22.

30. Sigmund Freud, *The Standard Edition of the Complete Psychological Works of Sigmund Freud*, vol. 18, *Beyond the Pleasure Principle, Group Psychology, and Other Works*, trans. James Strachey (Hogarth Press, 1966), 26.

31. As Bruno Latour writes, "Don't be fooled for a second by those who preach the call of wide-open spaces, of 'risk-taking,' those who abandon all protection and continue to point to the infinite horizon. . . . Those good apostles take risks only if their own comfort is guaranteed. Instead of listening to what they are saying about what lies ahead, look instead at what lies behind them: You'll see the gleam of the carefully-folded golden parachutes, of everything that ensures them against the random hazards of existence." Bruno Latour, *Down to Earth: Politics in the New Climatic Regime* (Polity, 2018), 11.

32. Primo Levi, *Survival in Auschwitz*, trans. Stuart Woolf (Simon & Schuster, 1996), 11, 56.

33. Arguably, this is the great difference between him and Rosenzweig/Levinas, who are easily intoxicated by the vertical.

34. "Most influential Jewish thinkers conceived of the intersubjective encounter, and therefore of the individuals who participate in it, in decidedly abstract terms. The 'other' they envisioned has no specific social location or set of needs. It is difficult, on the basis of these thinkers' writings, to imagine how such meetings occur in the course of ordinary life, and how duration of relationship, social proximity, and differences of power might affect them. An insistent tendency toward abstraction enabled these thinkers to argue for the universality of dyadic encounter and obligation." Mara Benjamin, *The Obligated Self: Maternal Subjectivity and Jewish Thought* (Indiana University Press, 2018), 13.

35. I can think of no better instantiation of this project in the contemporary world than Sloterdijk. Peter Sloterdijk, *Bubbles: Microspherology*, trans. Wieland Hoban, Spheres (Semiotext(e), 2011).

36. Buber, *I and Thou*, 59.

37. Dustin Atlas, "The Ark and Other Bubbles: Jewish Philosophy and Surviving the Disaster," *Religions* 13, no. 12 (2022): 2–10.

38. This is no doubt partly due to the infatuation with time (rather than space) that suffused German thought in the early twentieth century.

39. Again, see Mroczek, "Without Torah or Scripture."

40. Of course, they are joined in this by Hegel.

41. For a study of the inversion of this model, and the inversion of this inversion, see Silke Weineck, *The Tragedy of Fatherhood: King Laius and the Politics of Paternity in the West* (Bloomsbury Academic, 2014).

42. Much of this was conceived when my primary cat was "mine"—she and I traveled the world, and there was never any doubt who was responsible for her, and whom each of us favored. Now I have a family, and a cat in this place is a very different beast. Yes, I do all the feeding and cleaning and combing, but the cat has forged many relationships and clearly favors my son. I am not jealous of him. Or I try not to be.

43. Martin Buber, Zhuangzi, and Songling Pu, *Chinese Tales: Zhuangzi, Sayings and Parables and Chinese Ghost and Love Stories* (Humanities Press International, 1991), 111. For a complete English translation of the tales, see Pu Songling, *Strange Tales from Liaozhai*, trans. Sidney Sondergard, 6 vols. (Jain, 2008).

44. One frustrating thing about Buber is his steadfast refusal to delve into sexuality. So one might expect him to avoid the *Tales*' unseemly aspects, but he ends his introduction embracing them, even mocking their first English translation, which, "unfortunately omitted or paraphrased all passages that seemed... indecorous." While the most ribald tales don't make it into his selection, they are far less anodyne than Herbert Giles's earlier translation. Buber, Zhuangzi, and Pu, *Chinese Tales*, 113.

45. Martin Buber, *Hasidism and Modern Man* (Horizon Press, 1958), 116.

46. Buber, *Philosophical Interrogations*, 28.

2. Animals

1. In what follows, *animals* should be read as meaning "nonhuman animals"—obviously, humans are animals too, but common usage treats us otherwise.

2. Buber, *I and Thou*, 57.

3. This is part of the appeal of what Carl Sachs calls the "myth of the discursive given," or the error of assuming that the way we express ourselves is isometric to how we actually think (confusing discourse for cognition). I am concerned with the "myth of the spoken given," or the assumption that the words we use in conversation are the way we actually dialogue. Carl B. Sachs, "In Defense of Picturing; Sellars's Philosophy of Mind and Cognitive Neuroscience," *Phenomenology and the Cognitive Sciences* 18, no. 4 (2019): 670.

4. The fact that we agree on the words used for a situation does not mean that we agree, as we might have very different definitions of those words. The opposite can also be the case, where we have substantial agreement, but our words differ. This is noted in Mendelssohn, *Jerusalem*, 67.

5. Buber, *I and Thou*, 145.

6. We could draw no concept of dialogue—or indeed any concept—without language. Human collective action is largely unthinkable without speech. This collective action is the root of Arendt's notion of power in *On Violence* and is why she rejects any attempts to view human violence as "animal." Hannah Arendt, *On Violence* (Harcourt, Brace & World, 1970), 59–66.

7. I stay close to Deacon's Peircean thesis that humans use complex triadic symbol systems, and nonhumans primarily use indexes, which I explore below. There are, of course, nonlanguage-using humans who should not be stripped of their personhood. The division between language-using and nonlanguage-using should not be taken to map perfectly onto the human/nonhuman line. Terrence William Deacon, *The Symbolic Species: The Co-Evolution of Language and the Brain* (Norton, 1997), 21–28.

8. Deacon, *The Symbolic Species*, 22.

9. C. Hunger, *How Stella Learned to Talk: The Groundbreaking Story of the World's First Talking Dog* (HarperCollins, 2021). In popular books, this appeal is supported by an insurmountable amount of autobiographical data. The poorly named *How Stella Learned to Talk* (spoiler: She doesn't) is largely an account of the author's anxieties, including details about her apprehension about moving. I believe we are meant to identify first with the author and then with her general project. This is especially egregious given that the author's training (in human speech therapy) might allow her to help train nonhumans in speaking (maybe?), but it certainly does not help her evaluate them. There is no serious cognitive ethology referenced in the book, and the few notes refer to NPR, Napoleon Hill, and self-help texts more than any work on animal communication. I'm well aware this is a popular text, but given the number of footnotes, one would hope for more than a handful to refer to the supposed issue at hand.

10. As Slobodchikoff writes about animal language, "It's very controversial. That's because, according to many scientists and linguistic professionals, language is the last gulf that separates us from all of the other animals." This is "frightening to some people." It is true that animal language is controversial, but fear and difference are hardly the only reasons for the controversy. You can disagree without being a scaredy-cat. C. N. Slobodchikoff, *Chasing Doctor Dolittle: Learning the Language of Animals* (St. Martin's Press, 2012), 2.

11. Slobodchikoff, *Chasing Doctor Dolittle*, 3.

12. For this chapter, I lean heavily on the work of a teacher of mine, Kristen Andrews. This is not to saddle her with my positions, many of which she would no doubt disagree with. Kristen Andrews, *Do Apes Read Minds?: Toward a New Folk Psychology* (MIT Press, 2012).

13. I use *The Essential Peirce* for this book where I can because it includes the section numbers for the *Collected Papers*, which is, while more comprehensive, a mess. Charles S.

Peirce, *The Essential Peirce*, Vol. I (Indiana University Press, 1992), 225–27. Each of these signs corresponds to one of Peirce's metaphysical categories, which are firstness, secondness, and (unsurprisingly) thirdness. A basic formulation of this division can be seen as early as "On a New List of Categories" in Peirce, *The Essential Peirce*, 1–5.

14. Deacon, *The Symbolic Species*, 71.

15. Peirce, *The Essential Peirce*, 226.

16. This, like all summaries of Peirce's semiotics, is necessarily a simplification. It is necessary if only because Peirce's taxonomies changed so many times. Further, the function of an interpretant changes over his career. Arguably, indexes can "have" interpretants (a dynamic interpretant) insofar as they produce psychological effects, but this is a limited case—the main issue is that the symbol connects to multiple objects that can be different in kind.

17. Perhaps one of the most repellent elements of *How Stella Learned to Talk* is that Stella is treated as a human with a language learning disability—by a speech therapist, no less. Hunger, *How Stella Learned to Talk*.

18. Slobodchikoff, *Chasing Doctor Dolittle*, 43.

19. Deacon, *The Symbolic Species*, 13.

20. Animal studies, like religious studies, gender studies, and Jewish studies, is a collection of approaches to an object—not a unified body of work or method. It seeks to avoid anthropocentrism and anthropomorphism and give animals a place at the table. "Like trauma studies, gender studies, and postcolonial studies, animal studies stretches to the limit questions of language, epistemology, and ethics" by asking "how to understand and give voice to others or to experiences that seem impervious to our means of understanding; how to attend to difference without appropriating or distorting it; how to hear and acknowledge what it may not be possible to say." The book is thus close to animal studies, but it is not a member of the club because (following Buber) I am not interested in giving voice to the voiceless; I am far more interested in how we dialogue with animals. Kari Weil, found in Andrea Dara Cooper, "Writing Humanimals: Critical Animal Studies and Jewish Studies," *Religion Compass* 13, no. 12 (2019): e12341.

21. Counterintuitively, this will require that we stop calling Buber an ethicist, as *preexisting* ethical commitments can interfere with understanding relationships. Buber often ends up doing ethics, but he does not start there. Thus, Latour's question ("Where is the Levinas for animals?") has a complex answer. The answer, as Levinas well knew, is Buber, but the fundamental caveat for Levinas was that a relationship is necessarily ethical, whereas for Buber, something isn't ethical unless it's a relationship. B. Latour and C. Porter, *We Have Never Been Modern* (Harvard University Press, 1993), 136.

22. Note that a few pages later, he adopts a Deacon-lite position: [19] "Countless other species, such as dogs, rats and pigeons, have also learned to link a sign—such as a light or a movement—to an action; and it has not been shown convincingly that the ape-language of Washoe and Koko is any different qualitatively from this type of associative learning. . . . In comparison, a human two-year-old is able to use nouns, verbs, prepositions and so on, in a grammatically correct manner." Thus, he doesn't really grant animals humanlike language (as he shouldn't), but he is too comfortable allowing his projection to proceed (even though he knows it's false). Lars Svendsen, *Understanding Animals: Philosophy for Dog and Cat Lovers* (Reaktion Books, 2019), 12.

23. Svendsen, *Understanding Animals*, 22–23.

24. The unfortunately named "folk psychology" just means how we (or animals) think about other people's psyches and predict their behavior.

25. Andrews, *Do Apes Read Minds?*, 28.

26. Jeremy Bentham, *The Collected Works of Jeremy Bentham: An Introduction to the Principles of Morals and Legislation*, ed. J. H. Burns, H. L. A. Hart, and F. Rosen (Clarendon, 1996), 311n.

27. "Even without a robust understanding of beliefs and desires, agents can predict and explain others' behavior. They can also justify behavior, shape their own behavior to acceptable societal standards, coordinate their behavior with others, identify intentional action, make moral judgments, and engage in a host of other social practices that are arguably as important as predicting and explaining behavior." Andrews, *Do Apes Read Minds?*, 31, 184. It is worth noting that her antirepresentational stance brings her thought somewhat in line with Buber's.

28. Buber, *I and Thou*, 149.

29. Buber was not exactly a self-critical writer, and I am perhaps being too generous when I assume that the "as we usually do" applies to the first edition of *Ich und Du*.

30. Gilbert Simondon, *Two Lessons on Animal and Man*, trans. Drew Burk (University of Minnesota Press, 2015), 32.

31. Simondon, *Two Lessons on Animal and Man*, 36–37.

32. Bentham, *The Collected Works of Jeremy Bentham*, 283.

33. Montaigne is essentially a Renaissance figure in this typology. Bruno, one of Buber's subterranean influences, plays the role of a cosmological democrat, the result being that animals "should not be considered as inferior beings or caricatures of man." Simondon, *Two Lessons on Animal and Man*, 66.

34. Simondon, *Two Lessons on Animal and Man*, 70.

35. Simondon, *Two Lessons on Animal and Man*, 73.

36. On the question of animal pain, Descartes may equivocate, but he does not, for that reason, ever seem to allow the animal freedom. He rejects calling humans "rational animals" because he "would lapse from one question into two more difficult questions [what is an animal, and what is rational]—that they might be treated together is not a possibility." Jessica Riskin, *The Restless Clock: A History of the Centuries-Long Argument over What Makes Living Things Tick* (University of Chicago Press, 2016); R. Descartes and D. M. Clarke, *Meditations and Other Metaphysical Writings* (Penguin, 2003).

37. Our concepts and metaphors are informed by our labor practices. This is why Descartes's division is overcome not by philosophical acuity or even fashion, so much as a changing of the role animals play in our economy: "Eventually, Descartes's model was surpassed. In the first stages of the industrial revolution, animals were used as machines," but in time, they were replaced by steam and coal, and animals became "pets" and "livestock." John Berger, *Why Look at Animals?* (Penguin, 2009), 11.

38. Note that the folk remedy used in the book is just as cruel, without the benefit of Cartesianism. When injured and awaiting medicine, Maimon's family was told:

> We should make use of an easy household remedy. Someone should kill a dog, and I should put my injured foot into the body. Repeating this several times would definitely bring about some relief. His order was followed, with the success that we had hoped for. After several weeks, I could move my foot and put weight on it. My recovery continued until my foot was completely healed. I think that it wouldn't be a bad thing *if doctors paid more attention to household remedies*, for they are often used with great success in parts of the world without regular doctors and pharmacies.

Solomon Maimon, *The Autobiography of Solomon Maimon: The Complete Translation*, trans. Paul Reitter (Princeton University Press, 2020), 50–60 (emphasis added).

39. The debates over Buber's supposed Kantianism have been going on for so long that they are in danger of becoming a scholarly object. Steven Katz has famously claimed that Buber's thought depends on a Kantian metaphysics. I am sympathetic with Katz's critique of those who resist metaphysical analysis of Buber's metaphysics, but Katz overidentifies Buber's metaphysics with crude Kantianism. Katz (incorrectly) holds that Kant's noumenal is essentially like Buber's I-You, and the phenomenal is more or less "the entire basis" of Buber's I-It. Katz is confusing the fact that Kant and Buber are responding to similar problems with the notion that Buber is in some way merely repeating Königsberg. Such bifurcations are common in theological-philosophical discourse: One would need to show that they are formally similar, which he can't because they aren't.

Yes, Buber uses Kant's transcendental aesthetic at points in his thought. But Katz seriously overestimates the importance of this and, further, misreads Buber's philosophy of space and time. What is essential is that the It-World "hangs together" in space and time. Whether it does so because of the structure of appearances, the constitution of matter, or the straight-up enclosure in a universe-sized box, doesn't really matter.

Worse, Katz claims that the You-world follows the noumenal. Again, there are points of similarity, but the noumenal, for Kant's theoretical philosophy, is only accepted as a possibility; nothing can be further from Buber's You-world. The noumenal plays a greater role in Kant's ethics, but even here, the noumenal is determined by the structure of universal reason qua ethics: "the form of lawfulness in general." For Buber, this is not the case. The You-world is a world of singularities, with singular responses, and not universal laws. I am quite certain that Kant would dismiss Buber's You-relation as "enthusiasm." For his part, Buber explicitly and consistently rejects Kant's employment of bifurcation to deal with freedom, "to ascribe the existence of a thing so far as it is determinable in time . . . the law of natural necessity, only to appearance, and to ascribe freedom to the same being as a thing in itself." Steven T. Katz, "A Critical Review of Martin Buber's Epistemology of I-Thou," in *Martin Buber: A Centenary Volume*, ed. Jochanan Bloch Haim Gordan (KTAV, 1984); Katz, "Lawrence Perlman's 'Buber's Anti-Kantianism': A Reply," *AJS Review* 15, no. 1 (1990): 109–117.

40. Immanuel Kant, *Anthropology from a Pragmatic Point of View*, trans. R. B. Louden (Cambridge University Press, 2006), 168.

41. Of course, very few other animals cry, but wailing and whining are widespread. Michel de Montaigne, *The Complete Essays*, trans. M. A. Screech (Penguin, 2004), 511.

42. Kant, *Anthropology from a Pragmatic Point of View*, 90.

43. Mendelssohn holds that this recuperation of the body, as a thing with its own perfections, is the ground of the superiority of the moderns over the ancients. This is also true for Leibniz. Alexander Altmann, "Moses Mendelssohn on Education and the Image of Man," in *Studies in Jewish Thought: An Anthology of German Jewish Scholarship*, ed. Alfred Jospe (Wayne State University Press, 1981).

44. Kant, *Anthropology from a Pragmatic Point of View*, 90 (emphasis added).

45. Here, Buber and Heidegger, both drawing from Uexküll, end up with a similar distinction. But the distinction is drawn slightly differently: For Heidegger, the animal (unlike a rock) is open, but it lacks a world because it is not "disconcealed"; for Buber, the animal has relationships, but it can't set things at a distance. Their compensation prizes differ slightly: For Buber, animals get to have an environment and relationships within it; for Heidegger, the animals are "poor in world" but not absolutely worldless, as is the case with a rock or plastic toy. What the human has that the animal lacks is a lack (or distance). Both thinkers are

"guilty" of what Wolfe calls humanist conservatism: They attempt to restrict the "nothing," or the "empty," to human beings. I am not so sure this is a bad thing, insofar as the "nothing" or lack can be seen as a function of language. Wolfe, *Animal Rites*, 32; Giorgio Agamben, *The Open: Man and Animal*, trans. Kevin Attell (Stanford University Press, 2004), 55; Martin Buber, "Distance and Relation," in *The Knowledge of Man*, trans. Maurice S. Friedman (Harper & Row, 1965); Martin Heidegger, *The Fundamental Concepts of Metaphysics: World, Finitude, Solitude* (Indiana University Press, 1995), 186–200.

46. Buber, *I and Thou*, 84.
47. Kant, *Anthropology from a Pragmatic Point of View*, 91 (emphasis added).
48. de Montaigne, *The Complete Essays*, 505.
49. de Montaigne, *The Complete Essays*, 505.
50. He claims our actual behavior suggests that we all already know this: "How many ways we have of speaking to our dogs and they of replying to us! We use different languages again, and make different cries, to call birds, pigs, bulls and horses; we change idiom according to each species." de Montaigne, *The Complete Essays*, 512.

3. Domestic Cats

1. The answer? Eating mice, which are evil, causes the cat to forget.
2. As O'Connor writes of the archaeological evidence: The model of cat "domestication that emerges is of an uninvited dinner guest that became a tolerated lodger, and then a member of the family. This is uncontroversial." Terry O'Connor, *Animals as Neighbors: The Past and Present of Commensal Animals* (Michigan State University Press, 2013), 61.
3. O'Connor, *Animals as Neighbors*, 60.
4. Svendsen, *Understanding Animals*, 131.
5. Natsume Soseki, *I Am a Cat*, trans. Aiko Ito (Tuttle, 2011), 23.
6. A short list of cat works that investigate idiosyncrasy includes Smart's *My Cat Geoffrey*, Virginia Woolf's *Flush*, Natsume Soseki's *I Am a Cat*, Rilke and Baudelaire's poems, Sfar's *The Rabbi's Cat*, the panoply of writers in the Everyman's edition of *Cat Stories*, and a generous number of children's stories.
7. Adler's is by far the most (intentionally) ironic because she positions herself as a Buberian, but her cat is an anti-Buberian mystic. The cat thus seems to be more like the adolescent Buber, and Adler herself, an adult. "With the courtesy of a scholarly feline who knows that his Person has thought seriously about I and Thou, he gazed deeply into my eyes, just like the cat with whom Buber recounts such a moment in I and Thou. Then he briefly touched his nose to mine. I could only be moved at this acknowledgement of me and the theology of relationship I espouse, especially since the Mysticat, a committed acosmicist, believes that 'I' and 'thou' are illusory boundaries because we are all part of God." Rachel Adler, *Tales of the Holy Mysticat: Jewish Wisdom Stories by a Feline Mystic* (Banot Press, 2020).
8. Rosenzweig, in a letter criticizing Buber for an overly "philosophical" account of our relationships, reproaches Buber thus: "How glad you would be to incorporate Buddha into your paradise, that Eden of yours over which I-Thou stands written. How gladly you would let in the domestic cat and all the pious pagan souls. . . . But you don't manage to; in the end they only get as far as a lovely site in the antechamber to hell, as far as the It." Rosenzweig claims that Buber's work focuses on the relationship between the self and others, where

Rosenzweig would rather he begin with the relationship between the creator and the created. This (theological) move is unavailable to Buber, whose philosophical work relies on beginning from a phenomenological perspective (if only to undermine it) and so not assuming much about God or God's supposed relationships to other beings. Rosenzweig letter to Buber in Martin Buber, *The Letters of Martin Buber: A Life of Dialogue*, ed. Nahum N. Glatzer et al. (Schocken, 1991), l, 279.

9. Susan Tarcov, *Professor Buber and His Cats* (Lerner, 2022).

10. Paul Mendes-Flohr, *Martin Buber: A Life of Faith and Dissent* (Yale University Press, 2019), 55, 252.

11. Schalom Ben-Chorin, *The Other Martin Buber: Recollections of His Contemporaries*, ed. Haim Gordon (Ohio University Press, 1988), 163.

12. Buber, *I and Thou*, 144 (emphasis added).

13. As I interpret it, this dialogue is composed neither of symbols nor indexes. In Peircean language, this is an iconic sign, where the sign and its object are the same thing. This would mean, semiotically speaking, the sign overlaps the two dialogists. In a more material vein, it bears remembering that many animals don't like eye contact and consider it an act of aggression.

14. Buber, *I and Thou*, 145 (translation modified).

15. Buber, *I and Thou*, 145.

16. Once again, this line of thinking shows that Buber is often better seen as a post-post-Hegelian (after Kierkegaard and Feuerbach), rather than a neo-Kantian. Buber, *I and Thou*, 145 (emphasis added).

17. Buber's phenomenology does not allow a study of the ego (the "I") alone: the I is always in a relationship with an object or other subject, and it is changed by this object.

18. For Buber, language is able to take a becoming (say, the endless shifting colors that I see in a leaf) and give it stability by anchoring it to a symbol (the word *green*).

19. Buber, *I and Thou*, 145.

20. In Buber's own language, the "I" is always part of a ground word, and these ground words are word pairs (because they indicate a primal relationship).

21. The fact that Buber thinks such a relationship is possible completely disqualifies interpreters who want to view the I-You as a formal relationship where the parties can be interchanged. Because in a relationship like this one, only the human participant conceives of the relationship in these terms.

22. The second verse of Rilke's poem *Black Cat* takes a swipe at conceiving the way a cat "says" *you*, in visual terms:

> as if awakened, she turns her face to yours;
>
> and with a shock, you see yourself, tiny,
>
> inside the golden amber of her eyeballs
>
> suspended, like a prehistoric fly.

Rainer Maria Rilke, *The Selected Poetry of Rainer Maria Rilke*, bilingual ed., trans. Steven Mitchell (Knopf Doubleday, 1989), 65.

23. Buber, *I and Thou*, 146.

24. Walter Arnold Kaufmann, *Discovering the Mind*, 3 vols. (McGraw-Hill, 1980), vol. I, 263; Buber, *I and Thou*, 68, 89 (emphasis added).

25. Martin Heidegger, "Letter on 'Humanism,'" in *Pathmarks*, trans. Frank A. Capuzzi (Cambridge University Press, 1998), 239.

26. Domestically speaking, we can see this in the alternation between house and home.

27. Or worse, love is reserved for death-loving couples like Tristan and Isolde.

28. For Levinas, the origin of the ethical must be human—not the biological human, but the human as a category. In his attempt to present human life as a radical break from nature, as discontinuous with it, Levinas ends up restricting many phenomenological insights to human beings. Why? Because Levinas thinks in terms of species being, where humans are the species that is more than a species, the species of the face. So, when Levinas says, "Vegetarianism, for example, arises from the transference to animals of the idea of suffering. The animal suffers. It is because we, as human, know what suffering is that we can have this obligation," he is effectively restricting large swathes of phenomenology to the interhuman. I don't see an animal flail about, and then think via analogy with my own experience, "That looks like I would look if I were suffering," any more than I do with people. Rather, I see the animal's suffering directly. Levinas is aware of this, but he claims that the ability to see suffering as suffering (i.e., as a source of obligation) is developed first with other humans, and only later, via analogy, is it applied to animals. This position, where the human is not ontologically continuous with other animals, allows Levinas to say, "The widespread thesis that the ethical is biological amounts to saying that, ultimately, the human is only the last stage of the evolution of the animal. I would say, on the contrary, that in relation to the animal, the human is a new phenomenon. And that leads me to your question. You ask at what moment one becomes a face. I do not know at what moment the human appears, but what I want to emphasize is that the human breaks with pure being, which is always a persistence in being." This is an odd notion of Being. I suggest that Buber is correct, and that being enters the picture with language, which, because it can be iterated, introduces being into the flux of becoming. Emmanuel Levinas, "The Paradox of Morality: An Interview with Emmanuel Levinas," in *The Provocation of Levinas: Rethinking the Other*, ed. R. Bernasconi and D. Wood (Routledge, 1988), 172.

29. Emmanuel Levinas, "Martin Buber and the Theory of Knowledge," in *The Philosophy of Martin Buber*, ed. Paul Arthur Schilpp and Maurice S. Friedman (Open Court, 1967).

30. Levinas, "Martin Buber and the Theory of Knowledge," 145 (emphasis added).

31. Levinas, "Martin Buber and the Theory of Knowledge," 146.

32. The error here is rooted in a desire to see the highest in the lowest: If the goal of your thinking is ethical being, then there is a strong temptation to see elements of this ethics at the very basis of human being. But this is a conceit, or a preference. Buber's work offers an opening for ethical being; he does not specify that the building blocks themselves be ethical.

33. I would like to thank Crystal Clayville, who brought this passage to my attention.

34. Hans Jonas, *Philosophical Essays: From Ancient Creed to Technological Man* (Atropos Press, 2010), 245.

35. Jonas, *Philosophical Essays*, 246 (emphasis added).

36. Jonas, *Philosophical Essays*, 246. This is not entirely dissimilar from Peirce's position that indexical semiotics underpins symbolic systems.

37. Again, see Andrews, *Do Apes Read Minds?*.

38. Buber, *I and Thou*, 172.

39. Buber, *I and Thou*, 172.

40. I assume there are biological underpinnings here, but this is neither the point nor the criterion for the division. The house is.

41. Cooper, "Writing Humanimals." Derrida self-consciously echoes Buber when he invokes the irreducible singularity of his feline. I owe much of my thinking about the way the poetic operates in *The Animal* to Jonathan Luftig.

42. As when Derrida defends Buber in a footnote to the monstrous. Jacques Derrida, "Violence and Metaphysics," in *Writing and Difference*, trans. Alan Bass (Routledge, 2001), 401–2.

43. While Derrida frequently uses seemingly anti-Buberian language (such as his hostility to presence), his thought in aggregate does not reflect this. The above distinction between speech and language operates in Buber as well (again, dialogue can occur without content). And Derrida's critique of presence is a critique of a stable, accessible, and knowable presence that grounds claims. Buber, who is far more sanguine than Derrida about our ability to access the unmediated, nonetheless holds a similar position: For Buber, presence is very unstable (hence the cat's anxiety) and isn't a basis for about-statements.

44. Jacques Derrida, *The Animal That Therefore I Am*, trans. David Wills (Fordham University Press, 2009), 6.

45. I owe my understanding of the relationship among speech, text, and vision to Elliot Wolfson.

46. F. W. Nietzsche, *The Gay Science: With a Prelude in Rhymes and an Appendix of Songs*, trans. Walter Kaufmann (Vintage, 1974), sec. 352.

47. The Koren Talmud Bavli, Noé Edition (2020), Eruvin 100b.

48. Or, as per Rashi, "Whence has the knowledge come to you what shame there is in standing naked?"

49. There is supposedly something emancipatory about being nameless, and Cooper notes a possible parallel with Ursula K. Le Guin's "She Unnames Them," an untelling of Genesis 2:19 (and the naming of the animals): "'She Unnames Them' is an example of the kind of transformative storytelling Haraway envisions, offering a critique of naming practices in Genesis." Cooper, "Writing Humanimals."

50. Derrida, *The Animal That Therefore I Am*, 6. This might apply to Buber, but it is a rather unfair characterization of Rilke. Baudelaire's cat poem seems to me to just be about Baudelaire.

51. Derrida, *The Animal That Therefore I Am*, 7.

52. Derrida, *The Animal That Therefore I Am*, 9.

53. Derrida, *The Animal That Therefore I Am*, 13.

54. Derrida, *The Animal That Therefore I Am*, 14.

55. Derrida, *The Animal That Therefore I Am*, 32.

56. Rilke, *The Selected Poetry of Rainer Maria Rilke*.

57. For a thorough analysis of the limitations of the notion of projection, see Elliot R. Wolfson, *A Dream Interpreted Within a Dream: Oneiropoiesis and the Prism of Imagination* (Zone, 2011). The dream is a place where the boundary between the other and the self is stretched, and we encounter an other within, and the same without. A study of how much this provides a model for encounter or dialogue is a desideratum.

58. A forced conversant is not a partner in dialogue: I cannot make you dialogue with me. Buber claims that absence is part of the development, if not the structure, of a person; to meet someone, it must first be possible to miss-meet them. See the excellent and underread Phil Huston, *Martin Buber's Journey to Presence* (Fordham University Press, 2007).

59. Here, I (unsurprisingly) prefer Buberian terms and would distinguish between language and dialogue. To say animals use "language" is to employ a bizarre notion of language. I remain with my Deacon division: Animals use sign systems, but not symbolic languages. Finally, I would note that many cognitive ethologists, such as Andrews (see chap. 2), are well aware that the animal looks back and sees us seeing, hence the use of folk psychology.

60. Derrida, *The Animal That Therefore I Am*, 32.

61. This is perhaps easier to see with human beings. If I take someone seriously, as a person, I assume that some element of them is fundamentally hidden from me. Indeed, if someone appeared completely transparent to me, they would probably seem either inhuman or not human. Same with the animals: Derrida assumes (correctly, I think) that only an animal that can hide something is capable of entering into a relationship of response with us (and vice versa). Derrida's nakedness—his unconcealment—is a source of shame.

62. For the simplest presentation of this position, see Jacques Derrida, *Positions*, trans. A. Bass (Continuum, 2002), 22.

63. And of course, in this sense, unrepeatable in that the context that gives a phrase its meaning is always changing.

64. Derrida, *Positions*, 40, 49.

65. "I am afraid we are not getting rid of God because we still believe in grammar." Friedrich Wilhelm Nietzsche, *Twilight of the Idols, or, How to Philosophize with a Hammer*, trans. Duncan Large, Oxford World's Classics (Oxford University Press, 1998), Problem of Socrates sec. 6.

66. This is to be contrasted with Heidegger, for whom the poetry makes language *possible* (the poetic fact that language simultaneously conceals and reveals things, and that concealing and revealing are inextricably linked, is presupposed by the everyday). As Wolfson notes, "Language is not poetry because it is ur-poesy; rather, poesy happens in language because the latter preserves the primordial essence of poetry." And what is that primordial essence? Heidegger insists that language is not primarily a form of verbal communication based on words functioning as symbols signifying or representing beings extrinsic to the mind; "it is rather . . . the opening within which the giving is withheld, the revealing concealed, and the sayable unsaid. Language thus preserves the primacy of the event such that beings are disclosed in the nonbeing of the being of their nonbeing." This notion of the poetic has consequences for Heidegger's thinking about animals: "To the extent that Heidegger never abandoned the idea that language is the originary and hence distinctive essence of the being of human beings, and that without language there is no being and without being there is no language, his thought remains anthropocentric." Elliot R. Wolfson, *Heidegger and Kabbalah: Hidden Gnosis and the Path of Poiēsis* (Indiana University Press, 2019), 156, 302.

67. I would note the poetic and ecstatic are hardly immune from merely repeating prejudice, and many ravings are not the mark of inspiration but merely generations of bigotry taking flight.

68. The house of critical reasoning is built on a solid foundation of gossip. What are Freud and Nietzsche doing, if not systematizing the insights gleaned by gossip? This is why Nietzsche fears the wisdom of old women: It's his main competition.

69. Derrida, *The Animal That Therefore I Am*, 30 (emphasis added); in an anthropological key, Eduardo Kohn writes, "How other kinds of beings see us matters. That other kinds of beings see us changes things. If jaguars also represent us—in ways that can matter vitally to us—then anthropology cannot limit itself just to exploring how people from different societies might happen to represent them as doing so." Eduardo Kohn, *How Forests Think: Toward an Anthropology Beyond the Human* (University of California Press, 2013), 1. Kohn's interest here is the ways in which encounters are, but also are not, culturally contingent. The "universality" of some encounters is owed *not to a universal characteristic we share but to one shared by our partners in dialogue*. Kohn, *How Forests Think*, 1.

70. Derrida, *The Animal That Therefore I Am*, 31.
71. Derrida, *The Animal That Therefore I Am*, 40. I assume the irony of referring to "all philosophers" as those who treat animals as a homogeneous set did not escape Derrida.
72. Kieran Healy, "Fuck Nuance," *Sociological Theory* 35, no. 2 (2017): 118.
73. "Kinds are important to the agents and artisans.... Were not our world amenable to classification into kinds that we cognize, we should not have been able to develop any crafts ... 'natural kind' is a name for what helps people do better. Natural kinds, in short, seem important for homofaber." I am no doubt stretching Hacking's point—and perhaps your credulity. But a concept of dialogue that has no space for kinds will remain entirely restricted to the interhuman. Ian Hacking, "A Tradition of Natural Kinds," *Philosophical Studies: An International Journal for Philosophy in the Analytic Tradition* 61, nos. 1/2 (1991): 114.

4. Plants

1. Plato, *Phaedrus*, trans A. Nehamas and P. Woodruff (Hackett, 1995)230d.
2. Here, I follow Deacon and Peirce closely, where animals use nonarbitrary signs, firsts and seconds, icons and indexes—and humans use those but also thirds (symbols). Icons are signs that share characteristics with their referent (and can actually *be* their referent, as when things are signs of themselves), whereas the index is causally connected to its referent (as when smoke means fire).
3. Buber, *The Letters of Martin Buber*, 525.
4. David Chamovitz, *What a Plant Knows: A Field Guide to the Senses*, updated and expanded ed. (Farrar, Straus and Giroux, 2020), esp. chaps. 3 and 5.
5. As Marder notes, "The pulsations of vegetal temporality are often imperceptible to a conscious human observer, because even when they share a physical space, the two beings do not live in the same homogeneous time but are non-contemporaneous with one another." Michael Marder, *Plant-Thinking: A Philosophy of Vegetal Life* (Columbia University Press, 2013), 103.
6. Buber, *I and Thou*, 177, translation modified (emphasis added).
7. Here, the work of people like Marder and Jonas will help clarify this in a more material manner than Buber is capable of. Marder is very much influenced by Heidegger's phenomenology-ontology, and Jonas is more at home in the philosophy of life and biology. Marder's work has been invaluable for me, but I depart from his project on two counts. His work is primarily interested in what the plant does to and for philosophy. An important question, but not mine. My question is not interested in how plants can help us think but how we can dialogue with them. Also, Marder is animated by a concern for ethics.
8. Strauss presents an extreme example of the belief that the very idea of nature is Greek, holding (somewhat questionably) that "the concept of nature is foreign to the Bible" and "the prophets ... lack the idea of science and hence the idea of nature." Leo Strauss, ed., "Jerusalem and Athens: Some Introductory Reflections," in *Jewish Philosophy and the Crisis of Modernity* (SUNY, 1997), 377–405. Buber is far more Aristotelian than many realize, and it is worth noting that his first conception for a dissertation was to begin with Aristotle and end with Leibniz.
9. To be fair, it is extremely difficult to draw such a line. As Bergson notes, "No definite characteristic distinguishes the plant from the animal. Attempts to define the two kingdoms strictly have always come to naught. There is not a single property of vegetable life that is not

found, in some degree, in certain animals; not a single characteristic feature of the animal that has not been seen in certain species or at certain moments in the vegetable world." Drawing such a distinction depends, therefore, on tendencies and proportions. Bergson, like Aristotle, Buber, and countless others, ends up using locomotion as a criterion. Henri Bergson, *Creative Evolution*, trans. Irvin Edman (University Press of America, 1984), 118.

10. Marder notes that this duality is found in the word itself: "Vegetable means to be alive and to grow, whereas we use the word 'to vegetate' to suggest stasis." Marder, *Plant-Thinking*, 19.

11. Plato, *Timaeus*, trans. D. J. Zeyl (Hackett, 2000), 77bc.

12. Marder, *Plant-Thinking*, 59.

13. This is not a position I am willing to defend at length, but my job would be much easier if it were otherwise. See Chamovitz, *What a Plant Knows*, 66; Marder, *Plant-Thinking*, 50–55.

14. Bergson, *Creative Evolution*, 16. The plant, insofar as it is an individual at all, individuates in a very different manner than we do.

15. Interestingly, Buber sees this form of sign in Vaslav Nijinsky's dancing: "None of his gestures, to be sure, means anything other than itself. None refers to anything that is external to it." Martin Buber, "Brother Body," *Salmagundi*, nos. 33/34 (1976): 100.

16. Chamovitz, *What a Plant Knows*, 138 (emphasis added). Buber says something similar in his discussion of a linden tree (see below): "But the animal lives, as the biology of our day has recognized . . . 'with his environment as with his organs'; it perceives nothing more and nothing other than what and how the actual situation demands that it perceive. It enters into the functional circle and knows outside of its own needs and dangers hardly anything of other things and beings." Martin Buber, "Man and His Image Work," in *The Knowledge of Man*, 158.

17. Chamovitz, *What a Plant Knows*, 138 (emphasis added).

18. Marder, *Plant-Thinking*, 10.

19. Buber is aware of the difficulties surrounding silent dialogue, as the "two talks" in the *Eclipse of God* make quite clear: In the first talk, silence is oppressive—a product of Buber browbeating a man into agreeing with him.

20. Buber, *I and Thou*, 89.

21. Luce Irigaray and Michael Marder, *Through Vegetal Being: Two Philosophical Perspectives*, Critical Life Studies (Columbia University Press, 2016), 9–13.

22. Buber, *I and Thou*, 151 (emphasis added).

23. Buber, "Dialogue," 3.

24. Buber, "Dialogue," 5.

25. Irigaray and Marder, *Through Vegetal Being*, 3.

26. Levinas, "Martin Buber and the Theory of Knowledge," 136.

27. Levinas is correct when he writes, "Both the relation to things and the relation to man have something in common. Thus responsibility which we noted is at the basis of language, never assumes a strictly ethical import." He is wrong when he suggests this is a limitation. There is no a priori reason to assume sociality is either strictly human or that it is ethical. I suggest that neither phenomenology nor basic experiences are going to step into the breach here and take up arms for this position. Levinas's need to hijack relationality in the service of ethics might be morally efficacious, but it arbitrarily limits relationality to the narrow world of the interhuman. Relationality and sociality are necessary *conditions* for ethics, but it is difficult to say anything further than this without begging the question. Levinas, "Martin Buber and the Theory of Knowledge," 146.

28. Levinas, "Martin Buber and the Theory of Knowledge," 135.
29. Buber is not interested in the "totally other" as the totally other. For him, the partner in dialogue is both ephemeral and dependable. However, we can "translate" between Levinas's "totally other" and Buber's "You" with some success.
30. Levinas, "Martin Buber and the Theory of Knowledge," 134.
31. Levinas nonetheless views Buber as making the human the center of being in a way foreign to Buber's texts and intent: "If the notion of 'betweenness' functions as the fundamental category of being, however, man is the locus where the act of being is being acted Man must not be construed as a subject constituting reality but rather as the articulation itself of the meeting ... Man does not meet, he is the meeting ... Man is situated at the centre of being and philosophy is identifiable with anthropology." But Buber never says this. Indeed, he says the opposite: "I have never designated the between as 'the concept of the foundation and ultimate structure of being' ('le concept de base et la structure ultime de l'Etre'), nor have I ever understood it thus; I have only pointed out that we cannot do without this category for a full comprehension and presentation of what passes between two men when they stand in dialogue with each other." What's astonishing is not that Levinas makes this error but that it was perpetuated unthinkingly by Theunissen and many (otherwise excellent) interpreters. Buber, *Philosophical Interrogations*, 27; Levinas, "Martin Buber and the Theory of Knowledge," 140; Theunissen, *The Other*, 257–90.
32. That said, Margolin has shown that there is far more *Daniel* in *I and Thou* than many assume.
33. Martin Buber, *Daniel: Dialogues on Realization*, trans. M. Friedman (Syracuse University Press, 2018), 102–3. I am indebted to Zachary Braiterman for pointing this out to me.
34. Buber, *Daniel*, 47. Note that the translation of *dialogue* is *Gespräch*, not *Zwiesprache*, which is the title of Buber's later piece, "Dialogue."
35. Buber, *Daniel*, 54.
36. Buber, *Daniel*, 55. For a more sympathetic take on Buber's philosophy of unification, see Wolfson, "The Problem of Unity in the Thought of Martin Buber."
37. More kindly, one might see a parallel in what Buber calls the "elementary relational processes" of so-called primitive peoples. Buber, *I and Thou*, 56–70.
38. Huston, *Martin Buber's Journey to Presence*, 116.
39. This is, of course, a very questionable definition of mysticism. Paul R. Mendes-Flohr, *From Mysticism to Dialogue: Martin Buber's Transformation of German Social Thought* (Wayne State University Press, 1989).
40. Buber, *Daniel*, 55. A gender analysis of these passages is as desirable as it would be depressing. Beginning with the need for direction, it ends: "You come to the mother not otherwise than through the son," who is then compared to a sheath on a sword.
41. This all fits rather nicely in what Wolfson has called Buber's "existentialist" phase, where he introduces "decision (Entschlossenheit) [and] direction (Richtung)," in this case, embodied by the stick Buber presses against the tree in the preface. Wolfson, "The Problem of Unity in the Thought of Martin Buber."
42. Buber, *I and Thou*, 58.
43. Buber, *I and Thou*, 58.
44. Buber, *I and Thou*, 173.
45. The relationship between representation and speech in Buber is treated in Elliot R. Wolfson, "Theolatry and the Making-Present of the Nonrepresentable: Undoing (A) Theism in Eckhart and Buber," in *Martin Buber: His Intellectual and Scholarly Legacy*, ed.

Sam Shonkoff (Brill, 2018). Of absolute importance here is the paradox of personhood; in particular, that the imageless god is in fact an image, whereas the paradoxical application of personhood (which can be talked to) to the infinite is seen as a potential safeguard against turning the infinite into a thing (even an imageless thing).

46. Buber, "Man and His Image Work," 12.

47. Buber, "Man and His Image Work," 12.

48. N.b., for Jonas, metabolism is of greater importance for understanding life than DNA. See his appendix "Note on the Nonparticipation of DNA in Metabolism." For Jonas, all living beings exist in a relationship with death, or nonbeing, even if they don't "know" this: "Of all the polarities mentioned, most basic is that of being and not-being. From it, identity is wrested in a supreme, protracted effort of delay whose end is foredoomed: for not-being has generality, or the equality of all things, on its side. Its defiance by the organism must end in ultimate compliance, in which selfhood vanishes and as this unique one can never be retrieved." Hans Jonas, *The Phenomenon of Life: Toward a Philosophical Biology* (Northwestern University Press, 2001), 97.

49. There is no thought-in-itself because thought is developed out of shared symbol systems (something like an intellectual community in the abstract) and the related notion of objectivity, which occurs only when multiple agents relate to the same object and can communicate about it. However, as our concern is plants—who don't think in this sense—we can ignore this prong of his philosophy.

50. Here, Jonas continues a line of thought begun by Bergson. Jonas, *The Phenomenon of Life*, 99; Bergson, *Creative Evolution*, 124. My understanding of Hans Jonas is owed almost entirely to Ron Margolin.

51. Jonas, *The Phenomenon of Life*, 2.

52. As Marder notes, "Plant-thinking neither grasps its object—it has none!—nor impassively freezes in sheer inaction but instead operates by the multiplication of extensions, by contiguity with and by a meticulously adumbrated exposure to that which is materially thought in it. It matters little that vegetal life does not objectify what it strives toward . . . because it does not at the same time relate to itself." Marder, *Plant-Thinking*, 159.

53. Jonas, *The Phenomenon of Life*, 103.

54. This is not to discredit the important work of those who have noted far more similarities between plants and humans than the naked eye can see. While mutuality should not depend on mutual characteristics, it is nonetheless helpful to note that there are many. Plants and humans share a great deal of DNA, but they also sense characteristics. For instance, there are shared genes that regulate responses to light. Plants smell and use this sense to self-regulate (much as humans do, say, with menstruation). Finally, plants can not only feel touch, but in some cases, they can even "remember" this touch—even if this memory is entirely procedural. While none of these factors should determine our dialogues, and it's not clear this is more than a list of weird and wondrous characteristics, they do show that the absolute otherness of plants is overstated. Plants are radically (pardon the pun) other, but not completely so. Chamovitz, *What a Plant Knows*, 3, 38, 49, 123.

55. Incidentally, introducing semiotics to the plant world seems to me to be the value of Kohn's *How Forests Think*, as when he writes, "Contrary to our assumptions, representation is actually something more than conventional, linguistic, and symbolic. . . . Nonhuman life-forms also represent the world." This is valuable despite the book's (nonanthropocentric) idealism, as when Kohn writes things like "I want to show that the fact that we can make the claim that forests think is in a strange way a product of the fact that forests think. These two

things—the claim itself and the claim that we can make the claim—are related: It is because thought extends beyond the human that we can think beyond the human." The second half of this claim seems reasonable, depending on how one defines the term *extend*, but the first half's ready equation between the cognizable and the cognizing is an extremely questionable extension of Early Modern theology (however accidental). Kohn's idealism is purchased by claiming that all sign usage (including iconicity and indexicality) is a form of thinking. An argument can be made here (with the result that "thinking" will apply to more or less every being and process imaginable), but the link between thinking and thinkability is extremely tenuous: that if something is thinkable means that it is thinking, and this is questionable. For a thorough refutation of Kohn's position, see the excellent Graeber. Kohn, *How Forests Think*, 22; David Graeber, "Radical Alterity Is Just Another Way of Saying 'Reality': A Reply to Eduardo Viveiros de Castro," *HAU: Journal of Ethnographic Theory* 5, no. 2 (2015): 1–30.

56. Kohn, *How Forests Think*, 9.

57. Chamovitz, *What a Plant Knows*, 5: "Plants don't have a central nervous system; a plant doesn't have a brain that coordinates information for its entire body. Yet different parts of a plant are intimately connected, and information regarding light, chemicals in the air, and temperature is constantly exchanged between roots and leaves, flowers and stems, to yield a plant that is optimized for its environment."

58. Marder, *Plant-Thinking*, 84.

59. Chamovitz, *What a Plant Knows*, 4.

60. This debate operates in parallel to the issue of telos in biology, whether, as with Kant, we need to think about telos to make sense of life, or, as with Jonas and Deacon, we make the stronger claim that there is such a thing as naturalized (and therefore localized) telos in nature. In other words, where Kant says, "We need to think of lungs as being for breathing," then teleology is just a function of the limitations of our thinking. Whereas, when Jonas would say something like "Lungs are for breathing, that is part of what makes lungs what they are," then telos is part of the very structure of life. But, and this is important, it does not point to anything outside of the living processes it enables.

61. His book, which would have been better named *Biohermeneutics*, pulls together several threads to make the case that life is interpretive. I understand aesthetics may seem more expansive, and considering our shared sensoria, the case can be made for it, but what Strathausen adds to the discourse concerns interpretation more than it does sensation.

62. Carsten Strathausen, *Bioaesthetics: Making Sense of Life in Science and the Arts* (University of Minnesota Press, 2017), 24.

63. Strathausen, *Bioaesthetics*, 4.

64. See Eugene Thacker, *After Life* (University of Chicago Press, 2010).

65. Again, see Irigaray and Marder, *Through Vegetal Being*.

66. The archetypal example of this is Buber's abandonment by his mother, and the standard effect is alienation that allows you to individuate and better understand the stakes of encounter.

67. It died.

68. We will not treat this here, but I believe Marder is correct when he writes, "The aesthetic attitude, broadly conceived, seems to be more propitious to a nonviolent approach to plants than either their practical instrumentalization or their nominalist-conceptual integration into systems of thought." I am less interested in the ethics of this relation than he is, but I do think that the aesthetic has drawn more than one person into a relationship with the vegetal world. Marder, *Plant-Thinking*, 4.

69. Some forms of labor are more amenable to this directedness than others. Much of what goes by the name *alienation* is labor, where focus on the actual work is nearly impossible.
70. Voltaire, *Candide and Other Stories*, trans. Roger Pearson (Oxford University Press, 2006), 88.
71. Marder, *Plant-Thinking*, 8.
72. Buber, *Between Man and Man*, 211.

5. Babies

1. Anne O'Byrne, *Natality and Finitude* (Indiana University Press, 2010), 9.
2. Anna Freud, *Psychoanalysis for Teachers and Parents: Introductory Lectures* (Beacon, 1960), 28. Here, I follow the dated language used by the writers under discussion.
3. Charles Darwin, "A Biographical Sketch of an Infant," *Mind* 2, no. 7 (1877): 293.
4. Andrews, *Do Apes Read Minds?*, 24, 31.
5. This seems to be the cause of the contempt heaped on her by Lacanians who are allergic to any element of human being untied to language. Yet another case where the fans are worse than the band: Lacan himself had a productively ambivalent relationship with Klein, from whom he inherited the notion of a partial object. Jacques Lacan, "Some Reflections on the Ego," *International Journal of Psychoanalysis* 34 (1953): 11–17.
6. Buber, *I and Thou*, 62.
7. Buber, "Dialogue," 5 (emphasis added). I would have liked to omit the section deriding written language, but it is one of Buber's shortcomings, so it is best to see it and then explicitly reject it. Here, he joins Mendelssohn in preferring living speech to written language, which he considered to have a relationship much like a musical performance and the score. Elias Sacks, *Moses Mendelssohn's Living Script: Philosophy, Practice, History, Judaism* (Indiana University Press, 2017).
8. Buber, *I and Thou*, 89 (emphasis added).
9. Sex and gender present an obvious case: The supposed unmediated naturalness of sexual categories has been used to mask the machinations of power, or, as de Beauvoir snaps, "Is this attribute something secreted by the ovaries?" Simone de Beauvoir, *Le Deuxième Sexe* (Vintage, 1989), 13.
10. Buber, *I and Thou*, 62.
11. Buber, *I and Thou*, 63.
12. The key point here is not the particulars of how the market is supposed to be the best way of figuring out these conflicts but rather that the market, a mediating force, is viewed as a kind of stable information-processing regime. For a précis, see David Harvey, *A Brief History of Neoliberalism* (Oxford University Press, 2007). For an understanding of the philosophical and theological effects of neoliberalism, see the introduction in Adam Kotsko, *Neoliberalism's Demons: On the Political Theology of Late Capital* (Stanford University Press, 2018).
13. Derrida, because of his famous critique of presence, is often brought to bear against anyone who would speak of presence, but I am not sure Derrida does the work people want him to do. The thing Derrida calls *presence* is incredibly stable. And Buber's presence is many things, but it is profoundly, necessarily unstable. Buber's presence, I suggest, dodges many of Derrida's critiques because of its paradoxes and ephemeral nature. Good luck trying to build

something on top of it or using it to ground your claims. It might be the basis of a meaningful human life, but it is a base you cannot set anything on. Jacques Derrida, *Of Grammatology*, trans. G. C. Spivak (Johns Hopkins University Press, 2002), 12. For the classic, albeit heavy-handed, study of the ways presence is used to disguise ideology, see Theodor Adorno, *The Jargon of Authenticity* (Taylor & Francis, 2013), 11–12.
See Jacques Derrida, *Writing and Difference*, trans. Alan Bass (University of Chicago Press, 1978), esp. "Force and Signification."

14. And so, the baby is a problem for critical thought. Critical thinking, which decomposes seemingly simple entities to reveal the political, economic, and libidinal forces structuring them, is an affair for mature persons and well-composed subjectivities: Critical thought is a game of "heads," a function of thought. "In the dialogue of heads, only head theories will ever come up." Peter Sloterdijk, *Critique of Cynical Reason*, Theory and History of Literature, vol. 40 (University of Minnesota Press, 1987), 104. Buber's insistence that the head cannot be separated from the body without spiritual repercussions finds an echo in his criticism of Zalman's Chabad:

> This very name, which detaches the specifically intellectual Sefirot out of the closely linked structure, points to the principle underlying this school: reason and intellect are to be reinstated as a way to find God. . . . The very separating off of the spheres threatened to deprive Hasidism of its strongest base: the teaching that sparks of God are inherent in all things and creatures, in all concepts and urges, sparks which desire us to redeem them and, linked with this teaching, the affirmation of the soul-body entity of man, provided he is able to turn all his stirrings toward God.

Martin Buber, *Tales of the Hasidim*, trans. Olga Marx (Knopf Doubleday, 1991).

15. Philosophers are frequently guilty of claiming that all people are equal but then limiting what "counts" as a person. The game goes like this: People are equal, but the proper person is a rational agent. From there, I need only declare women, Jews, blacks, or whoever to not be rational, and then I have reinstated a hierarchy under the cover of equality.

16. Johannes Wolfgang von Goethe, *Faust I & II*, vol. 2: *Goethe's Collected Works—Updated edition*, trans. S. Atkins and D. E. Wellbery (Princeton University Press, 2014), 152.

17. This is perhaps why thinkers often try to claim the baby, assuming the baby's-eye-view provides evidence for a preferred metaphysics: "A child is by definition not yet that which it alone has the capacity to become. It is in this unique capacity to become. It is in this unique capacity, in this potential, I suggest, that the child's availability—and so too its value as a cultural resource—lies." Claudia Castañeda, *Figurations: Child, Bodies, Worlds* (Duke University Press, 2002); Mara Benjamin, "Intersubjectivity Meets Maternity: Buber, Levinas, and the Eclipsed Relation," in *Thinking Jewish Culture in America*, ed. Kenneth Koltun-Fromm (Lexington Books, 2013).

18. See Cooper, *Gendering Modern Jewish Thought* as a presentation of gender in the surrounding culture (especially Rosenzweig). Even Buber's Zionism was shaped by the loss of the mother: "It is up to us to make the world reliable again for the children. It depends on us whether we can say to them and to ourselves: 'Don't worry. Mother is here.'" Martin Buber, "The Children," in *Men of Dialogue: Martin Buber and Albrecht Goes*, ed. William Rollins and Harry Zohn and trans. Harry Zohn (Funk & Wagnalls, 1969), 228.

19. Distancing is treated in his paper "Distance and Relation." It concerns the human ability to set things at a distance, including the "I." Miss-meeting—best theorized by Huston—is found in the opening section of Buber's 1960 semiautobiographical collection of fragments, *Meetings: Autobiographical Fragments* [*Begegnung: autobiographische Fragmente*], regarding

a reunion with his mother: "When after another twenty years I again saw my mother, who came from a distance to visit me, my wife, and my children, I could not look into her still astonishingly beautiful eyes without hearing from somewhere the word 'Vergegnung' as a word spoken to me." Buber writes that this word *mis-meeting [Vergegnung]* "designate[s] the failure of a real meeting among men," but what matters for us is that it creates a space for the identification of discrete objects (Its) and a discrete "I." Martin Buber, *Meetings: Autobiographical Fragments*, trans. Maurice S. Friedman (Routledge, 2002).

20. Buber, *I and Thou*, 76.
21. Buber, *I and Thou*, 76.
22. Psychoanalysis, at least in the '20s, focused more on the trauma of birth, given its most extreme formulation by Otto Rank and preserved in a more moderate form by Melanie Klein.
23. Freud's story of individuation told at the outset of *Civilization and Its Discontents* occurs after birth, but there, it is assumed that the infant, like the fetus, cannot yet distinguish between itself and the surrounding world. Sigmund Freud, *Civilization and Its Discontents*, trans. James Strachey (Norton, 2010), chap. 1.
24. Buber, *I and Thou*, 76.
25. Sloterdijk, *Bubbles*, 293.
26. Buber holds that the natal relation without subject or object develops into a "drive to relation": "The innateness [*Ursprünglichkeit*] of the longing for relation [*Beziehungstrebens*] is apparent even in the earliest and dimmest stage. Before any particulars can be perceived, dull glances push into the unclear space toward the indefinite . . . [this is] not experience of an object." Instead of an object relation, we have a preobject drive. Buber, *I and Thou*, 78.
27. Buber, *I and Thou*, 77 (emphasis added).
28. Buber, *I and Thou*, 78 (emphasis added). The translation here is unfortunate, as Buber does not seem to care much about panpsychism one way or the other, and he has an actual affection for non-Idealist forms of pantheism. For a study of the all-too-quick allergy expressed toward pantheism, see Mary Jane Rubenstein, *Pantheologies: Gods, Worlds, Monsters* (Columbia University Press, 2018).
29. Buber, *I and Thou*, 78 (emphasis added).
30. Darwin, "A Biographical Sketch of an Infant."
31. Part of this capriciousness is their proximity to speech: They improve as they age and develop an acquaintance with language long before they can be said to really dwell in it (to say nothing of reading and writing). There is no clear path here. One of my son's first words was *thermostat*, much to the delight of his caregiver.
32. Klein assumes the primacy of biological motherhood and the importance of breastfeeding looms large in her work. I have no interest in strengthening the Natural Baby Industrial Complex and have, if anything, an animosity toward it. I am not going to "correct" her work but rather take it at its word and assume the reader can correct for contemporary sensibilities.
33. Melanie Klein, *Autobiography* (Melanie Klein Trust, 1959).
34. Melanie Klein, "On Weaning," in *Love, Guilt and Reparation and Other Works 1921–1945* (Random House, 2011), 290. She argues in "Development of a Child" that child therapy is an inevitable outcome of Freud's work: "The possibility and necessity of analysing children is an irrefutable deduction from the results of analyses of adult neurotics, which always trace back into childhood the causes of illness," Melanie Klein, ed., "Development of a Child," in *Love, Guilt and Reparation and Other Works 1921–1945* (Random House, 2011), 25.
35. Freud, *Civilization and Its Discontents*, 72.

36. Julia Kristeva, *Melanie Klein* (Columbia University Press, 2001), 12.

37. The first is a serious concern; the latter is beneath contempt.

38. There is a problem with any purely theoretical employment of psychoanalytic texts: psychoanalysis is therapeutic; academic work is not. Psychoanalytic theory has its own criteria: Truth is a by-product of, and enables, a practice. Thus, in psychoanalysis, theory and practice are intertwined in a way that they aren't for most other academic discourses.

39. Again, I follow Klein's language and tendencies here, both in terms of the primacy of the breast over the bottle and her assumption that mothers are in charge of the feeding process. I am fully aware (in theory and in practice) that neither of these can or should be assumed. I trust we are all able and willing to bring Klein into the present by both understanding her concepts in a more general manner than intended and by correcting against her chauvinism (much as one day, someone will correct against ours).

40. "Notes on Some Schizoid Mechanisms (1946)," in Melanie Klein, *Envy and Gratitude and Other Works 1946–1963* (Random House, 2011), 2.

41. Eva Brann, *The Ways of Naysaying: No, Not, Nothing, and Nonbeing* (Rowman & Littlefield, 2001), 9–20.

42. Klein, "On Weaning," 308–13.

43. Klein, "On Weaning," 290.

44. Klein, "On Weaning," 290 (Klein's emphasis).

45. Klein, *Envy and Gratitude and Other Works*, 62.

46. Klein, *Envy and Gratitude and Other Works*, 63.

47. Freud, *Psychoanalysis for Teachers and Parents*, 29: "The child who has left his infancy and his first year behind him suddenly learns that his mother does not belong to him alone."

48. Buber, "Brother Body," 99.

49. Klein, *Envy and Gratitude and Other Works*, 122. Play technique is not the best evidence for relationships like dialogue because it assumes such relationships from the outset. It is, however, an extraordinary method for investigating them.

50. Klein, *Envy and Gratitude and Other Works*, 126.

51. Susan Sherwin-White, "Melanie Klein and Infant Observation," *Infant Observation* 20, no. 1 (2017): 1–22.

52. Hans Gadamer, *Truth and Method*, trans. J. Weinsheimer and D. G. Marshall (Bloomsbury Academic, 2013), 109.

53. Gadamer, *Truth and Method*, 107: "Play has its own essence, independent of the consciousness of those who play. Play—indeed, play proper—also exists when the thematic horizon is not limited by any being-for-itself of subjectivity, and where there are no subjects who are behaving 'playfully.'"

54. Babies are manipulative because their reach exceeds their grasp. They need things, desperately, that they have no power to get themselves, and they cannot simply ask for them.

55. Klein, *Envy and Gratitude and Other Works*, 123.

56. This technique suggests a theory of language where words, too, are objects, which might be troubling to some. More to the point, it does help determine the way to Klein's theory of object relations.

57. Klein, *Envy and Gratitude and Other Works*, 128.

58. Darwin, "A Biographical Sketch of an Infant," 292.

59. Buber, "The Children," 225.

60. Buber, "On Education," in *Between Man and Man*, 107.

61. Melanie Klein, *Love, Guilt and Reparation and Other Works 1921–1945* (Random House, 2011), 1.

6. Sensuality

1. For models of a pluralist pantheism (one where enough difference between entities is preserved to allow for dialogue), see Rubenstein, *Pantheologies*, 17–25, 168–71.
2. Buber, "Dialogue," 14.
3. Margaret Olin has also convincingly argued that Buber's "use of formal analysis to create a place for Jewish art" informs his later dialogical writings, and so, in turn, his philosophy of relations. Certainly, Buber's interest in relations and their importance for his philosophy are evident in his early art writings. Margaret Rose Olin, *The Nation Without Art: Examining Modern Discourses on Jewish Art*, Texts and Contexts (University of Nebraska Press, 2001), 103–6.
4. Martin Buber, "Jewish Renaissance," in *The First Buber: Youthful Zionist Writings of Martin Buber*, ed. and trans. G. G. Schmidt (Syracuse University Press, 1999), 30, 34; Buber, "Jewish Artists," in *The First Buber*, 101. For the most thorough treatment of the Jewish Renaissance, see Asher Biemann, *Inventing New Beginnings: On the Idea of Renaissance in Modern Judaism* (Stanford University Press, 2009). For a cursory treatment of Buber's early aesthetic theories, see Marcia Allentuck, "Martin Buber's Aesthetic Theories: Some Reflections," *Journal of Aesthetics and Art Criticism* 30, no. 1 (1971): 35–38.
5. For a study of the grip Michelangelo had on modern Jewish thinkers, see Asher Biemann, *Dreaming of Michelangelo: Jewish Variations on a Modern Theme* (Stanford University Press, 2012). According to Braiterman, *Gestalt* has a central place in Buber's work by 1912, whereas he is more ambivalent about form and formation in his piece on Lesser Ury in 1903. Zachary Braiterman, *The Shape of Revelation: Aesthetics and Modern Jewish Thought* (Stanford University Press, 2007), 33–34.
6. Michael Berkowitz, *Zionist Culture and West European Jewry Before the First World War* (University of North Carolina Press, 1996), 132.
7. Buber, "Jewish Artists," 30.
8. There are instead "artists who in their being and in their works express Jewish ethnicity." Martin Buber, "Lesser Ury," in *The First Buber*, 65.
9. Buber, "Lesser Ury," 65.
10. Buber, "Lesser Ury," 65. As Braiterman has noted, the word Buber uses in this 1903 paper is *Form*, not *Gestalt* (which has a more positive valence for him).
11. Buber, *I and Thou*, 57. Note that the "Imageless God" is still an image (the image of the imageless).
12. Buber, *I and Thou*, 57 (emphasis added).
13. Buber, "Lesser Ury," 83.
14. This form of pantheism does not eradicate singular beings; it merely connects them. See Rubenstein, *Pantheologies*. Lesser Ury is not alone here. In Buber's brilliant "Brother Body," a paper celebrating the famous dancer Vaslav Nijinsky, Buber is even more explicit about the creative value of movement and its relationship to play and art. Buber, "Lesser Ury," 83; Buber, "Brother Body."
15. Buber, "Man and His Image Work," 150.

16. Buber, "Man and His Image Work," 151.

17. Buber, "Man and His Image Work," 151. Note that this passage ends with a phrase that recalls Leibniz's dictum "Nothing is in the intellect that was not first in the senses, except the intellect itself." This phrase famously found itself in the frontispiece of Wundt's "Contributions on the Theory of Sensory Perception." Jochen Fahrenberg, "The Influence of Gottfried Wilhelm Leibniz on the Psychology, Philosophy, and Ethics of Wilhelm Wundt" (2017), https://doi.org/10.6094/UNIFR/12694 (emphasis added).

18. Buber, "Man and His Image Work," 156.

19. Buber, "Man and His Image Work," 150.

20. Buber, "Man and His Image Work," 156.

21. Buber, "Man and His Image Work," 157.

22. See Wolfson, "Theolatry and the Making-Present of the Nonrepresentable."

23. Names, of course, offer another dimension on this problem. They suggest more intimacy with and knowledge of the person or object than the bare pronoun does. But not much more.

24. Buber, "Man and His Image Work," 157 (emphasis added). The transcendental x is treated by Kant in *Critique of Pure Reason*, A150. Its role is as a marker for the "something" that the understanding links appearances to. It is thus something "of which we can know nothing at all." Note that for Kant, Buber's operation wouldn't work because "this transcendental object cannot even be separated from the sensible data, for then nothing would remain through which it would be thought." This would not bother Buber, for whom the fact that the x partakes in the production of sense data is a general characteristic of all sensual objects. Despite the efforts of many commentators, Buber is not a Kantian. Kant is, for Buber, a source for forms and images of thought. Immanuel Kant, *Critique of Pure Reason*, trans. Paul Guyer and Allen W. Wood (Cambridge University Press, 1998), A150.

25. Buber is here, as elsewhere, closer to being a post-post-Hegelian (following Kierkegaard and Feuerbach) than he is to being a post-Kantian.

26. Buber, "Man and His Image Work," 158. Buber uses this difference apologetically (between imitation and those who seek to maintain the dialectic between the invisible and the visible) to distinguish between Pauline Christianity and so-called Pharisaic Judaism. Martin Buber, *Two Types of Faith* (Collier, 1986), 130. Wolfson, in his seminal *Speculum*, demonstrates that visibility of the invisible is an essential problem that spurs many forms of Jewish mysticism, several of which operate in the background of Buber's work. Elliot R. Wolfson, *Through a Speculum That Shines: Vision and Imagination in Medieval Jewish Mysticism* (Princeton University Press, 1994).

27. Buber, "Man and His Image Work," 158.

28. This is most emphatically not to say that all sensation is reciprocal or dialogical, only that it can be. It is an interaction between the "I" on one side, and, on the other, an "x."

29. Scholem, who refused to concede that Buber ever moves beyond his early period, famously held that Buber's dynamics have two principles "the formless and the formative ... that which has been formed [*Geformte*] never remains pure form [*Gestalt*], and again and again the formless [*Gestaltlosen*] breaks in and breaks up the form [*Form*]." This reading informs the many erroneous readings of Buber where form is "bad." Braiterman corrects Scholem's interpretation, noting that for Buber, there is a normative distinction between two types of form: *Gestalt* has an affirmative, productive valence, while *Form* is detrimental to life. Thus, there are two types of distinction: one between *Form* and *Gestalt*, and, within *Gestalt*, one between the formative [*Gestaltende*] and formless [*Gestaltlosen*], where both

"work in league" to "undermine the kingdom of rotting *Gestalt*." Gershom Gerhard Scholem, "Martin Buber's Concept of Judaism," in *On Jews and Judaism in Crisis* (Schocken, 1976), 136; Braiterman, *The Shape of Revelation*, 33 Buber, *I and Thou*, 61 (translation modified).

30. Michelangelo's *Slaves* exerted a pull over countless thinkers and has been enlisted in support of nearly every possible aesthetic theory. Buber is no exception here. For a treatment of Buber's relationship to the Renaissance sculptor, see Biemann, *Dreaming of Michelangelo*, 101–2. However, Biemann does have an unfortunate tendency to paper over the change in Buber's thinking about form and creation, which is easily rectified by a reading of Braiterman. Braiterman, *The Shape of Revelation*, 33–34.

31. Buber, "Man and His Image Work," 150.

32. Buber, "Man and His Image Work," 150.

33. Buber, "What Is Man?," in *Between Man and Man*[o], 141.

34. Buber, in turn, accuses Kant of raising an important question but not answering it because Kant focuses on what humans do, not what they are. This is not unfair. As Alix Cohen has noted, Kant "redirects the question 'what is man?' from defining man in terms of what he is to defining him in terms of what he does," but Buber considers this redirection to be a misdirection. Alix Cohen, "Kant's Answer to the Question 'What Is Man?' and Its Implications for Anthropology," *Studies in History and Philosophy of Science* 39 (2009): 506–14 (emphasis added).

35. Buber, "What Is Man?," 194.

36. Following Erlewine's reading strategy, we could say that many of Buber's war works are engaged in a hidden polemic against Heidegger and other Nazi philosophers, and that much that seems apologetic is in fact polemics. R. Erlewine, *Judaism and the West: From Hermann Cohen to Joseph Soloveitchik* (Indiana University Press, 2016).

37. Buber, "What Is Man?," 199. For a historical study of Buber's relation to Heidegger, see Paul Mendes-Flohr, "Martin Buber and Martin Heidegger in Dialogue," *Journal of Religion* 94, no. 1 (2014): 2–25. For a detailed take on the philosophical relationship between the two, see Herskowitz, *Heidegger and His Jewish Reception*.

38. Heidegger's account of tools appeared in print in 1927, between *I and Thou* and "What Is Man?"

39. Buber, "What Is Man?," 211. Gregory Kaplan first made me aware of the importance of the everyday for Buber. See "Derrida's Cat" in chapter 3 for an extended discussion of the everyday and Heidegger.

40. Buber, "What Is Man?," 213.

41. Buber, "What Is Man?," 210 (translation modified).

42. The accuracy of Buber's presentation of Hasidic sources forms the subject of an exhausting debate. What is certainly the case is that the texts collected in *Hasidism and Modern Man* use sources selected and translated to make a very specific set of points, and it should not be assumed they present a model of Hasidism that would pass muster with an anthropologist or sociologist, to say nothing of a philologist.

43. Buber, *Hasidism and Modern Man*, 33.

44. Buber, *Hasidism and Modern Man*, 55.

45. Buber, *Hasidism and Modern Man*, 174.

46. Buber, *Hasidism and Modern Man*, 174.

47. Whether Buber reads Hasidic sources with the intention of finding his philosophy in them or if his philosophy is inspired by them, I leave to scholars of Hasidism.

48. Again, note that this chapter is only treating one kind of awareness (*Innewerdens*); namely, sensuality. An account of imagination or, say, mathematical intuition, would proceed very differently.

49. Adorno, *The Jargon of Authenticity*, 12.

50. In Buber's more dramatic language, the I-x is expressed in the craft relation by "realiz[ing] the perfection of the relation to the substratum of the sense things: through the figuration in the vision and in work. He [sic] does not portray the form, he does not really mould it . . . he pushes [*treibt*] it into its perfection in its fully figured reality." Buber, "Man and His Image Work," 164 (translation modified).

51. Herschel B. Chipp and Paul Klee, eds., *Theories of Modern Art: A Source Book by Artists and Critics* (University of California Press, 1984), 182. For the definitive treatment of Klee and modern Jewish thought, see Braiterman, *The Shape of Revelation*.

52. Buber, "Distance and Relation," 65. Here, Buber is clearly echoing but attempting to repudiate Heidegger.

53. Buber, "Distance and Relation," 65.

54. "Es ist ein Bild von etwas und von nichts; mag seine ein Zeichen, aber auch sein Urheber weiß Nicht, war es bezeichnen soll." Buber, "Distance and Relation," 66 (emphasis added, translation modified).

55. Buber, "Distance and Relation," 66.

56. Buber, *Philosophical Interrogations*, 66.

57. "der Niederschlag der Beziehung des Menschen zu den Dingen." Buber, "Distance and Relation," 66.

58. E. H. Gombrich, *The Sense of Order: A Study in the Psychology of Decorative Art*, 2nd ed. (Phaidon, 1984), 241.

59. Paul Klee, *The Diaries of Paul Klee, 1898–1918* (University of California Press, 1968), 8.

60. "If there is one psychological disposition about which one can afford to be dogmatic it is our readiness to see faces in any configuration which remotely suggests the presence of eyes and corresponding features." Gombrich, *The Sense of Order*, 265.

61. For a peerless treatment of these works, see Jurgis Baltrušaitis, *Aberrations: An Essay on the Legend of Forms* (MIT Press, 1989).

62. Baltrušaitis, *Aberrations*, 70.

63. Examples of this work abound, but perhaps the largest archive of such material-driven forms is found in medieval grotesques: "For the masters of the grotesque, interpretation of accidental shapes and contours always played an essential role. Monsters engraved on ancient gems and creatures on medieval margins illustrate this process which seems to lie between daydream and poetry." Ewa Kuryluk, *Salome and Judas in the Cave of Sex: The Grotesque: Origins, Iconography, Techniques* (Northwestern University Press, 1987), 305.

BIBLIOGRAPHY

Adler, Rachel. *Tales of the Holy Mysticat: Jewish Wisdom Stories by a Feline Mystic.* Banot Press, 2020.
Adorno, Theodor. *The Jargon of Authenticity.* Taylor & Francis, 2013.
Agamben, Giorgio. *The Open: Man and Animal.* Translated by Kevin Attell. Stanford University Press, 2004.
Allentuck, Marcia. "Martin Buber's Aesthetic Theories: Some Reflections." *Journal of Aesthetics and Art Criticism* 30, no. 1 (1971): 35–38.
Altmann, Alexander. "Moses Mendelssohn on Education and the Image of Man." In *Studies in Jewish Thought: An Anthology of German Jewish Scholarship*, edited by Alfred Jospe. Wayne State University Press, 1981.
Andrews, Kristen. *Do Apes Read Minds?: Toward a New Folk Psychology.* MIT Press, 2012.
Arendt, Hannah. *The Human Condition.* 2nd ed. Translated by M. Canovan. University of Chicago Press, 2013.
Arendt, Hannah. *On Violence.* Harcourt, Brace & World, 1970.
Aristotle. *Politics: A New Translation.* Translated by C. D. C. Reeve. Hackett, 2017.
Atlas, Dustin. "The Ark and Other Bubbles: Jewish Philosophy and Surviving the Disaster." *Religions* 13, no. 12 (2022): 1152.
Atlas, Dustin. "How to Do Things with Things: Craft at the Edge of Buber's Philosophical Anthropology." [In English.] *IMAGES* 12, no. 1 (2019): 134–47.
Bakhtin, Mikhail. *Problems of Dostoevsky's Poetics.* Translated by C. Emerson. University of Minnesota Press, 1984.
Baltrušaitis, Jurgis. *Aberrations: An Essay on the Legend of Forms.* MIT Press, 1989.
Benjamin, Mara. "Intersubjectivity Meets Maternity: Buber, Levinas, and the Eclipsed Relation." In *Thinking Jewish Culture in America*, edited by Kenneth Koltun-Fromm. Lexington Books, 2013.
Benjamin, Mara. *The Obligated Self: Maternal Subjectivity and Jewish Thought.* Indiana University Press, 2018.
Bentham, Jeremy. *The Collected Works of Jeremy Bentham: An Introduction to the Principles of Morals and Legislation.* Edited by J. H. Burns, H. L. A. Hart, and F. Rosen. Clarendon, 1996.
Berger, John. *Why Look at Animals?* Penguin, 2009.
Bergson, Henri. *Creative Evolution.* Translated by Irvin Edman. University Press of America, 1984.
Berkowitz, Michael. *Zionist Culture and West European Jewry before the First World War.* University of North Carolina Press, 1996.
Biemann, Asher. *Dreaming of Michelangelo: Jewish Variations on a Modern Theme.* Stanford University Press, 2012.
Biemann, Asher. *Inventing New Beginnings: On the Idea of Renaissance in Modern Judaism.* Stanford University Press, 2009.
Braiterman, Zachary. *The Shape of Revelation: Aesthetics and Modern Jewish Thought.* Stanford University Press, 2007.

Brann, Eva. *The Ways of Naysaying: No, Not, Nothing, and Nonbeing*. Rowman & Littlefield, 2001.
Buber, Martin. *Between Man and Man*. Routledge Classics. Routledge, 2002.
Buber, Martin. "Brother Body." *Salmagundi*, nos. 33/34 (1976): 98–101.
Buber, Martin. "The Children." In *Men of Dialogue: Martin Buber and Albrecht Goes*. Translated by Harry Zohn. Funk & Wagnalls, 1969.
Buber, Martin. *Daniel: Dialogues on Realization*. Translated by M. Friedman. Syracuse University Press, 2018.
Buber, Martin. "Dialogue." In *Between Man and Man*. Routledge, 2002.
Buber, Martin, ed. "Distance and Relation." In *The Knowledge of Man*. Translated by Maurice S. Friedman. . Harper & Row, 1965.
Buber, Martin. *Hasidism and Modern Man*. Horizon Press, 1958.
Buber, Martin. *I and Thou*. Translated by Walter Arnold Kaufmann. Scribner, 1970.
Buber, Martin, ed. "Jewish Artists." In *The First Buber: Youthful Zionist Writings of Martin Buber*. Translated by G. G. Schmidt. Syracuse University Press, 1999.
Buber, Martin, ed. "Jewish Renaissance." In *The First Buber: Youthful Zionist Writings of Martin Buber*. Translated by G. G. Schmidt. Syracuse University Press, 1999.
Buber, Martin, ed. "Lesser Ury." In *The First Buber: Youthful Zionist Writings of Martin Buber*. Translated by Gilya Schmidt. Syracuse University Press, 1999.
Buber, Martin. *The Letters of Martin Buber: A Life of Dialogue*. Edited by Nahum N. Glatzer, Paul R. Mendes-Flohr, Richard Winston, Clara Winston, and Harry Zohn. Schocken, 1991.
Buber, Martin, ed. "Man and His Image Work." In *The Knowledge of Man*. Translated by Maurice S. Friedman. Harper & Row, 1965.
Buber, Martin. *Meetings: Autobiographical Fragments*. Translated by Maurice S. Friedman. Routledge, 2002.
Buber, Martin. "On Education." In *Between Man and Man*. Routledge, 2002.
Buber, Martin. *Philosophical Interrogations: Interrogations of Martin Buber, John Wild, Jean Wahl, Brand Blanshard, Paul Weiss, Charles Hartshorne, Paul Tillich*. Edited by Sydney Chester Rome and Beatrice K. Rome. Holt, 1964.
Buber, Martin. *Tales of the Hasidim*. Translated by Olga Marx. Knopf Doubleday, 1991.
Buber, Martin. *Two Types of Faith*. Collier, 1986.
Buber, Martin. "What Is Man?" In *Between Man and Man*. Routledge, 2002.
Buber, Martin, Zhuangzi, and Songling Pu. *Chinese Tales: Zhuangzi, Sayings and Parables and Chinese Ghost and Love Stories*. Humanities Press International, 1991.
Carlin, George. *Back in Town*. Atlantic, 1996. Sound recording, 1 sound disc: digital; 4 3/4 in., 92728-2 Atlantic.
Carson, Maria. "The Emotional Heschel." PhD diss., Syracuse University, 2021. https://surface.syr.edu/etd/1422/.
Castañeda, Claudia. *Figurations: Child, Bodies, Worlds*. Duke University Press, 2002.
Chamovitz, David. *What a Plant Knows: A Field Guide to the Senses*. Updated and expanded ed. Farrar, Straus and Giroux, 2020.
Chipp, Herschel B., and Paul Klee, eds. *Theories of Modern Art: A Source Book by Artists and Critics*. University of California Press, 1984.
Cohen, Alix. "Kant's Answer to the Question 'What Is Man?' and Its Implications for Anthropology." *Studies in History and Philosophy of Science* 39 (January 1, 2009): 506–14.

Cooper, Andrea Dara. *Gendering Modern Jewish Thought*. Indiana University Press, 2021.
Cooper, Andrea Dara. "Writing Humanimals: Critical Animal Studies and Jewish Studies." *Religion Compass* 13, no. 12 (2019): e12341.
Darwin, Charles. "A Biographical Sketch of an Infant." *Mind* 2, no. 7 (1877): 285–94.
Deacon, Terrence William. *The Symbolic Species: The Co-Evolution of Language and the Brain*. Norton, 1997.
de Beauvoir, Simone. *Le Deuxième Sexe*. Vintage, 1989.
Deleuze, G., and F. Guattari. *A Thousand Plateaus: Capitalism and Schizophrenia*. Athlone Press, 1988.
de Montaigne, Michel. *The Complete Essays*. Translated by M. A. Screech. Penguin, 2004.
Dennett, D. C. *Intuition Pumps and Other Tools for Thinking*. Norton, 2013.
Derrida, Jacques. *The Animal That Therefore I Am*. Translated by David Wills. Fordham University Press, 2009.
Derrida, Jacques. *Of Grammatology*. Translated by G. C. Spivak. Johns Hopkins University Press, 2002.
Derrida, Jacques. *Positions*. Translated by A. Bass. Continuum, 2002.
Derrida, Jacques. "Violence and Metaphysics." In *Writing and Difference*. Translated by Alan Bass. Routledge, 2001.
Derrida, Jacques. *Writing and Difference*. Translated by Alan Bass. University of Chicago Press, 1978.
Descartes, R., and D. M. Clarke. *Meditations and Other Metaphysical Writings*. Penguin, 2003.
Dworkin, Andrea. *Right-Wing Women: The Politics of Domesticated Females*. Women's Press, 1983.
Erlewine, R. *Judaism and the West: From Hermann Cohen to Joseph Soloveitchik*. Indiana University Press, 2016.
Fahrenberg, Jochen. "The Influence of Gottfried Wilhelm Leibniz on the Psychology, Philosophy, and Ethics of Wilhelm Wundt." 2017. https://doi.org/10.6094/UNIFR/12694.
Fonrobert, Charlotte. *Menstrual Purity: Rabbinic and Christian Reconstructions of Biblical Gender*. Stanford University Press, 2002.
Freud, Anna. *Psychoanalysis for Teachers and Parents: Introductory Lectures*. Beacon, 1960.
Freud, Sigmund. *Civilization and Its Discontents*. Translated by James Strachey. Norton, 2010.
Freud, Sigmund. *The Standard Edition of the Complete Psychological Works of Sigmund Freud*. Vol. 18, *Beyond the Pleasure Principle, Group Psychology, and Other Works*. Translated by James Strachey. Hogarth Press, 1966.
Gadamer, Hans. *Truth and Method*. Translated by J. Weinsheimer and D. G. Marshall. Bloomsbury Academic, 2013.
Gombrich, E. H. *The Sense of Order: A Study in the Psychology of Decorative Art*. 2nd ed. Phaidon, 1984.
Graeber, David. "Radical Alterity Is Just Another Way of Saying 'Reality': A Reply to Eduardo Viveiros De Castro." *HAU: Journal of Ethnographic Theory* 5, no. 2 (2015): 1–41.
Habermas, Jürgen. "A Philosophy of Dialogue." In *Dialogue as a Trans-Disciplinary Concept*, edited by Paul Mendes-Flohr. Martin Buber's Philosophy of Dialogue and Its Contemporary Reception. De Gruyter, 2015.
Hacking, Ian. "A Tradition of Natural Kinds." *Philosophical Studies: An International Journal for Philosophy in the Analytic Tradition* 61, nos. 1/2 (1991): 109–26.

Harvey, David. *A Brief History of Neoliberalism*. Oxford University Press, 2007.
Harvey, Warren Zev. "Jewish Philosophy for the Twenty-First Century: Personal Reflections." In *Jewish Philosophy Tomorrow: Post-Messianic and Post-Lachrymose*, edited by Hava Tirosh-Samuelson and Aaron W. Hughes. Brill, 2014.
Healy, Kieran. "Fuck Nuance." *Sociological Theory* 35, no. 2 (2017): 118–27.
Heidegger, Martin. *The Fundamental Concepts of Metaphysics: World, Finitude, Solitude*. Indiana University Press, 1995.
Heidegger, Martin, ed. "Letter on 'Humanism.'" In *Pathmarks*. Translated by Frank A. Capuzzi. Cambridge University Press, 1998.
Herskowitz, Daniel. *Heidegger and His Jewish Reception*. Cambridge University Press, 2020.
Heschel, Abraham. *The Sabbath*. Farrar, Straus and Giroux, 2005.
Horwitz, Rivka, and Martin Buber. *Buber's Way to "I and Thou": The Development of Martin Buber's Thought and His "Religion as Presence" Lectures*. 1st American ed. Jewish Publication Society, 1988.
Hunger, C. *How Stella Learned to Talk: The Groundbreaking Story of the World's First Talking Dog*. HarperCollins, 2021.
Huston, Phil. *Martin Buber's Journey to Presence*. Fordham University Press, 2007.
Imhoff, Sarah. "Homemaking in Palestine: Jessie Sampter, Religion, and Relation." In *At Home and Abroad*, edited by Hurd Elizabeth Shakman and Sullivan Winnifred Fallers. Columbia University Press, 2021.
Irigaray, Luce, and Michael Marder. *Through Vegetal Being: Two Philosophical Perspectives*. Critical Life Studies. Columbia University Press, 2016.
Jonas, Hans. *The Phenomenon of Life: Toward a Philosophical Biology*. Northwestern University Press, 2001.
Jonas, Hans. *Philosophical Essays: From Ancient Creed to Technological Man*. Atropos Press, 2010.
Kant, Immanuel. *Anthropology from a Pragmatic Point of View*. Translated by R. B. Louden. Cambridge University Press, 2006.
Kant, Immanuel. *Critique of Pure Reason*. Translated by Paul Guyer and Allen W. Wood. Cambridge University Press, 1998. https://www.loc.gov/catdir/description/cam028/97002959.html.
Katz, Claire. *Levinas, Judaism, and the Feminine: The Silent Footsteps of Rebecca*. Indiana University Press, 2003.
Katz, Steven T. "A Critical Review of Martin Buber's Epistemology of I-Thou." In *Martin Buber: A Centenary Volume*, edited by Jochanan Bloch Haim Gordan. KTAV, 1984.
Katz, Steven T. "Lawrence Perlman's 'Buber's Anti-Kantianism': A Reply." *AJS Review* 15, no. 1 (1990): 109–17.
Kaufmann, Walter Arnold. *Discovering the Mind*. 3 vols. McGraw-Hill, 1980.
Kavka, Martin. "Verification (Bewährung) in Martin Buber." [In English.] *Journal of Jewish Thought and Philosophy* 20, no. 1 (2012): 71–98.
Kierkegaard, Søren. *Concluding Unscientific Postscript to the Philosophical Crumbs*. Translated by Alastair Hannay. Cambridge Texts in the History of Philosophy. Cambridge University Press, 2009.
Kierkegaard, Soren. *The Point of View*. Translated by H. V. Hong and E. H. Hong. Princeton University Press, 1998.
Klee, Paul. *The Diaries of Paul Klee, 1898–1918*. University of California Press, 1968.

Klein, Melanie. *Autobiography*. Melanie Klein Trust, 1959.
Klein, Melanie. "Development of a Child." In *Love, Guilt and Reparation and Other Works 1921–1945*. Random House, 2011.
Klein, Melanie. *Envy and Gratitude and Other Works 1946–1963*. Random House, 2011.
Klein, Melanie. *Love, Guilt and Reparation and Other Works 1921–1945*. Random House, 2011.
Klein, Melanie. "On Weaning." In *Love, Guilt and Reparation and Other Works 1921–1945*. Random House, 2011.
Kohn, Eduardo. *How Forests Think: Toward an Anthropology Beyond the Human*. University of California Press, 2013.
Kotsko, Adam. *Neoliberalism's Demons: On the Political Theology of Late Capital*. Stanford University Press, 2018.
Kristeva, Julia. *Melanie Klein*. Columbia University Press, 2001.
Kuryluk, Ewa. *Salome and Judas in the Cave of Sex: The Grotesque: Origins, Iconography, Techniques*. Northwestern University Press, 1987.
Lacan, Jacques. "Some Reflections on the Ego." *International Journal of Psychoanalysis* 34 (1953): 11–17.
Latour, B., and C. Porter. *We Have Never Been Modern*. Harvard University Press, 1993.
Latour, Bruno. *Down to Earth: Politics in the New Climatic Regime*. Polity, 2018.
Lehman, M. *Bringing Down the Temple House: Engendering Tractate Yoma*. Brandeis University Press, 2022.
Levenson, J. D. *Creation and the Persistence of Evil: The Jewish Drama of Divine Omnipotence*. Princeton University Press, 1994.
Levi, Primo. *Survival in Auschwitz*. Translated by Stuart Woolf. Simon & Schuster, 1996.
Levinas, Emmanuel. *Difficult Freedom: Essays on Judaism*. Johns Hopkins Jewish Studies. Johns Hopkins University Press, 1990.
Levinas, Emmanuel. "Martin Buber and the Theory of Knowledge." In *The Philosophy of Martin Buber*, edited by Paul Arthur Schilpp and Maurice S. Friedman. Open Court, 1967.
Levinas, Emmanuel. "The Paradox of Morality: An Interview with Emmanuel Levinas." In *The Provocation of Levinas: Rethinking the Other*, edited by R. Bernasconi and D. Wood. Routledge, 1988.
Levitt, Laura. *Jews and Feminism: The Ambivalent Search for Home*. Routledge, 1997.
Long, Christopher. "A Fissure in the Distinction: Hannah Arendt, the Family and the Public/Private Dichotomy." *Philosophy & Social Criticism* 24, no. 5 (1998): 85–104.
Maimon, Solomon. *The Autobiography of Solomon Maimon: The Complete Translation*. Translated by Paul Reitter. Princeton University Press, 2020.
Marder, Michael. *Plant-Thinking: A Philosophy of Vegetal Life*. Columbia University Press, 2013.
McKeon, Michael. *The Secret History of Domesticity: Public, Private, and the Division of Knowledge*. Johns Hopkins University Press, 2006.
Mendelssohn, Moses. *Jerusalem: Or on Religious Power and Judaism*. Translated by Allan Arkush. Brandeis University Press, 1983.
Mendes-Flohr, Paul. *Martin Buber: A Life of Faith and Dissent*. Yale University Press, 2019.
Mendes-Flohr, Paul. "Martin Buber and Martin Heidegger in Dialogue." *Journal of Religion* 94, no. 1 (2014): 2–25.
Mendes-Flohr, Paul R. *From Mysticism to Dialogue: Martin Buber's Transformation of German Social Thought*. Wayne State University Press, 1989.

Mroczek, Eva. "Without Torah or Scripture: Biblical Absence and the History of Revelation." *Hebrew Studies* 61 (2020): 97–122.
Nietzsche, Friedrich Wilhelm. *The Gay Science: With a Prelude in Rhymes and an Appendix of Songs*. Translated by Walter Kaufmann. Vintage, 1974.
Nietzsche, Friedrich Wilhelm. *Twilight of the Idols, or, How to Philosophize with a Hammer*. Translated by Duncan Large. Oxford World's Classics. Oxford University Press, 1998.
O'Byrne, Anne. *Natality and Finitude*. Indiana University Press, 2010.
O'Connor, Terry. *Animals as Neighbors: The Past and Present of Commensal Animals*. Michigan State University Press, 2013.
Olin, Margaret Rose. *The Nation without Art: Examining Modern Discourses on Jewish Art*. Texts and Contexts. University of Nebraska Press, 2001.
Peirce, Charles S. *The Essential Peirce*. Indiana University Press, 1992.
Perlman, Lawrence. "Buber's Anti-Kantianism." *AJS Review* 15, no. 1 (1990): 95–108.
Peskowitz, M. B. *Spinning Fantasies: Rabbis, Gender, and History*. University of California Press, 2023.
Plato. *Phaedrus*. Translated by A. Nehamas and P. Woodruff. Hackett, 1995.
Plato. *Timaeus*. Translated by D. J. Zeyl. Hackett, 2000.
Rilke, Rainer Maria. *The Selected Poetry of Rainer Maria Rilke*. Bilingual ed. Translated by Steven Mitchell. Knopf Doubleday, 1989.
Riskin, Jessica. *The Restless Clock: A History of the Centuries-Long Argument over What Makes Living Things Tick*. University of Chicago Press, 2016.
Rosenzweig, Franz. *The Star of Redemption*. Translated by Barbara E. Galli. Modern Jewish Philosophy and Religion. Translations and Critical Studies. University of Wisconsin Press, 2005.
Rubenstein, Mary Jane. *Pantheologies: Gods, Worlds, Monsters*. Columbia University Press, 2018.
Sachs, Carl B. "In Defense of Picturing; Sellars's Philosophy of Mind and Cognitive Neuroscience." *Phenomenology and the Cognitive Sciences* 18, no. 4 (2019): 669–89.
Sacks, Elias. *Moses Mendelssohn's Living Script: Philosophy, Practice, History, Judaism*. Indiana University Press, 2017.
Scholem, Gershom Gerhard, ed. "Martin Buber's Concept of Judaism." In *On Jews and Judaism in Crisis*. Schocken, 1976.
Sherwin-White, Susan. "Melanie Klein and Infant Observation." *Infant Observation* 20, no. 1 (2017): 5–26.
Simondon, Gilbert. *Two Lessons on Animal and Man*. Translated by Drew Burk. University of Minnesota Press, 2015.
Slobodchikoff, C. N. *Chasing Doctor Dolittle: Learning the Language of Animals*. St. Martin's Press, 2012.
Sloterdijk, Peter. *Bubbles: Microspherology*. Translated by Wieland Hoban. Spheres. Semiotext(e), 2011.
Sloterdijk, Peter. *Critique of Cynical Reason*. Theory and History of Literature. Vol. 40. University of Minnesota Press, 1987.
Songling, Pu. *Strange Tales from Liaozhai*. Translated by Sidney Sondergard. 6 vols. Jain, 2008.
Soseki, Natsume. *I Am a Cat*. Translated by Aiko Ito. Tuttle, 2011.
Strathausen, Carsten. *Bioaesthetics: Making Sense of Life in Science and the Arts*. University of Minnesota Press, 2017.

Strauss, Leo. "Jerusalem and Athens: Some Introductory Reflections." *Commentary* (1967): 13.
Svendsen, Lars. *Understanding Animals: Philosophy for Dog and Cat Lovers*. Reaktion Books, 2019.
Tarcov, Susan. *Professor Buber and His Cats*. Lerner, 2022.
Thacker, Eugene. *After Life*. University of Chicago Press, 2010.
Thalos, M. *Without Hierarchies: The Scale Freedom of the Universe*. Oxford University Press, 2013.
Theunissen, Michael. *The Other: Studies in the Social Ontology of Husserl, Heidegger, Sartre, and Buber*. MIT Press, 1984.
Tronto, J. C. *Moral Boundaries: A Political Argument for an Ethic of Care*. Routledge, 1993.
Voltaire. *Candide and Other Stories*. Translated by Roger Pearson. Oxford University Press, 2006.
von Goethe, Johannes Wolfgang. *Faust I & II*. Vol. 2, *Goethe's Collected Works*. Updated ed. Translated by S. Atkins and D. E. Wellbery. Princeton University Press, 2014.
Weineck, Silke. *The Tragedy of Fatherhood: King Laius and the Politics of Paternity in the West*. Bloomsbury Academic, 2014.
Wittgenstein, Ludwig. *Tractatus Logico-Philosophicus*. Translated by Michael Beaney. Oxford University Press, 2023.
Wolfe, Cary. *Animal Rites: American Culture, the Discourse of Species, and Posthumanist Theory*. University of Chicago Press, 2008.
Wolfson, Elliot R. *Circle in the Square: Studies in the Use of Gender in Kabbalistic Symbolism*. State University of New York Press, 1995.
Wolfson, Elliot R. *A Dream Interpreted Within a Dream: Oneiropoiesis and the Prism of Imagination*. Zone, 2011.
Wolfson, Elliot R. *Heidegger and Kabbalah: Hidden Gnosis and the Path of Poiēsis*. Indiana University Press, 2019.
Wolfson, Elliot R. "The Problem of Unity in the Thought of Martin Buber." *Journal of the History of Philosophy* 27, no. 3 (1989): 424.
Wolfson, Elliot R. "Theolatry and the Making-Present of the Nonrepresentable: Undoing (a) Theism in Eckhart and Buber." In *Martin Buber: His Intellectual and Scholarly Legacy*, edited by Sam Shonkoff. Brill, 2018.
Wolfson, Elliot R. *Through a Speculum That Shines: Vision and Imagination in Medieval Jewish Mysticism*. Princeton University Press, 1994.

INDEX

absence 7–8, 90, 52n58
Adam 50, 53
Adler, Rachel 40, 40n7
Adorno, Theodor 106
aesthetics 5, 74, 76, 97, 102, 106
Agamben, Giorgio 145
Andrews, Kristin 32–34, 78, 123
animal 11, 13, 15, 24–38, 40–48, 50–53, 55–62, 91
anthropocentrism 3, 33, 62, 32n20, 54n66
anthropomorphism 3, 43, 62, 32n20
anxiety 13, 26, 40–44, 47–48, 56
Arendt, Hannah 16–17, 16n6
Aristotle 12, 15, 18–19, 47, 60, 60n8
art 95, 97–99, 102–106, 108–110, 97n4
attention 1–3, 32, 34, 41–43, 75–76, 2n5, 15n2

babies 3, 77–81, 86, 88–93, 113
Bakhtin, Mikhail 10n31
Baltrušaitis, Jurgis 109
Baudelaire, Charles 51, 50n50
Beauvoir, Simone de 80n9
Benjamin, Mara 92, 21n34
Bentham, Jeremy 33
Berger, John 35, 35n37
Bergman, Hugo 58–59
Bergson, Henri 61, 60n9
betweenness 64n31
Bible 19, 50, 99, 103
birds 11, 24
birth 77–78, 87, 89, 93, 139
Braiterman, Zachary 97, 102, 97n5, 102n21
breastfeeding 86–90, 85n32, 88n39
bubbles 4, 22, 79

Candide 75
care 4, 15, 78, 111, 16n2
Carlin, George 9
Carson, Maria 19
cat 1, 23, 25–26, 38–53, 55–57, 59, 77, 79

Chamovitz, David 61, 72n59
children 16, 36, 73, 75, 78, 81–93, 81n17, 81n18
Cooper, Andrea 50n49
crafts 95–97, 99, 102–109, 106n50

Dajani family 40
Daniel 65–66
Darwin, Charles 78, 86, 93
Deacon, Terrence 27, 29, 71, 27n7
death 4, 9, 26, 72–73, 78, 95–96, 111–113, 69n48
decoration 96, 102–103, 106–108, 110
Deleuze, Gilles 39, 10n28
Derrida, Jacques 47–57, 80, 48n41, 53n61, 80n13
Descartes, René 35–36, 52, 35n36, 35n37
domestic 4, 9, 12, 14–24, 34, 39, 41, 48, 55, 65, 73, 75, 77, 81, 93–94, 105, 109
domestication 15, 17, 39, 41, 47–48
Dworkin, Andrea 12, 18, 20n29

eruv 19, 130
ethics 16, 24, 27–28, 34, 45–46, 53, 64, 71, 32n21, 19n26, 46n32, 64n27
everyday 8, 53–55, 76, 104, 54n66
existentialism 62, 66n41

family 16, 84, 90, 93, 39n2
father 17, 22, 83, 19n24
Freud, Sigmund 17, 19–20, 22, 24, 43, 50, 61, 71, 78, 82, 86–87, 92, 55n68, 83n23

Gadamer, Hans 91
garden 24, 60–61, 63–64, 73–76
Genesis 18, 53, 99, 103, 50n49
ghosts 23
God and gods 21, 40, 48, 50, 53, 62, 68, 93, 98–100, 103, 6n16, 40n8, 68n45
Goethe, Johann Wolfgang von 69, 83
Gombrich, Ernst 108
gossip 4, 23, 55, 65, 55n68

153

Index

Habermas, Jürgen 9, 9n25
Haraway, Donna 39, 50n49
Hasidism 11, 22–24, 27, 59, 105
Hegel, Georg 62
Heidegger, Martin 53–54, 76, 78, 104, 5n13, 19n26, 38n45, 54n66
hermeneutics 47, 71–72, 87, 92, 95
Herskowitz, Daniel 5n13
Heschel, Abraham 19, 10n28
Heschel, Susannah, 10n28
Hitchcock, Alfred 17, 22
home 4, 12, 15–24, 48, 54, 64, 73–74, 77, 84, 93, 111
humanism 37–38, 62, 38n45
Husserl, Edmund 75
Huston, Phil 66, 82n19

icons 29, 31, 40, 61, 77–78, 40n13, 58n2
I-It 7–8, 43, 82, 10n31, 38n39
imagination 3, 67, 84–85, 89
Imhoff, Sarah 15
in-between 5, 82–83, 107, 5n13
index 3, 29–31, 42, 49, 61, 77–78
infants 36, 77–78, 82–89, 92, 94
Irigaray, Luce 64
irritability 69–71
I-You 2, 4–8, 11–12, 43–47, 56, 58, 60, 64, 74, 76, 82, 95, 99, 101, 43n21

Jewish 1, 12–15, 17–19, 21–22, 47, 71, 86, 97
Jonas, Hans 46–47, 69–72, 92, 59n7, 69n48, 72n60

Kant 34, 36–38, 100–101, 104, 36n39, 72n60, 101n24, 104n34
Kaplan, Gregory 8n21, 102n39
Kaufmann, Walter 44
Kavka, Martin 5n14
Kierkegaard 49, 3n9, 101n25
Klee, Paul 106, 108–109
Klein, Melanie 22, 24, 79, 82, 84, 86–94, 79n5, 88n39
Kohn, Eduardo 71, 55n69, 71n55
Kristeva, Julia 87

labor 9, 95, 111, 35n37
Lacan, Jacques 52, 79n5

Latour, Bruno 20n31, 32n21
Leibniz, Gottfried Wilhelm 7, 37, 60n8, 99n17
Levinas, Emmanuel 18–19, 45–46, 48, 62, 64–65, 19n26, 32n21, 34n28, 64n31
Levitt, Laura 12, 18, 6n17

Maimon, Salomon 35, 36n38
Mendelssohn, Moses 16n7, 80n7
metabolism 36, 69, 71–72, 69n48
Michelangelo 97, 102
Montaigne, Michel de 35–38, 50
mothers 78, 81–84, 86–90, 66n40, 73n66
Mroczek, Eva 17

names 9, 42, 50, 55, 83, 50n49, 101n23
natality 78, 82–83
Nietzsche, Friedrich 50, 54, 91, 102
Nijinsky, Vaslav 61n15, 98n14
nothing 7, 27, 65, 85, 103, 107–108, 38n45

object-relations 88
organism 9, 20–21, 56, 70, 72, 113
otherness 45, 62, 70, 75, 85, 99, 105, 71n54
O'Byrne, Anne 77

panpsychism 85
pan-relation 85
pantheism 98, 82n28, 141
Peirce, Charles 3, 28–29, 40, 61, 71, 6n14, 40n13, 58n2
pets 16, 24, 32, 62, 10n28, 35n27
phenomenology 46, 60–62, 75, 42n17, 45n28, 64n27
plant 3, 11, 24, 47, 58–66, 68–76, 86, 113, 10n31, 59n70, 61n16
Plato 2, 60
play 38, 86, 90–94
pointing 3–4, 21, 30, 42, 49, 78
prelinguistic 13, 63, 72, 77, 80, 89, 91–92, 94
pronouns 3, 29, 42–43, 101
psychoanalysis 20, 71, 83, 87, 90–93, 83n22, 87n38

reciprocity 1–3, 5, 45–47, 52, 59–60, 67–69, 71, 74, 82–83, 85, 90, 95–96, 98, 104–106, 109–110, 101n28, 10n31

Rilke, Rainer Maria 51–52, 43n22
Rosenzweig, Franz 19, 40, 21n33, 40n8

Scholem, Gershom 102n29
sensation 37, 69–70, 85, 89, 95–97, 99–104, 106, 108–109
sexuality 15, 17, 22–23, 89, 93, 23n44
signals 26, 29–31, 42, 47, 66, 77, 113
signs 29–31, 52, 58, 61, 71, 78–80, 40n13
silence 12, 23, 63–65, 77, 80, 63n18
Simondon, Gilbert 34–36, 55
singularities 7, 37–39, 42, 44, 49–51, 55–57, 61, 101, 107, 109, 36n39, 98n14
Slobodchikoff, Constantine 31, 27n10
Sloterdijk, Peter 84, 21n35
Socrates 34
Songling, Pu 23
Soseki, Natsume 39
species 24, 31–33, 39, 43, 46–47, 51, 67, 45n28
Strathausen, Carsten 72
Strauss, Leo 60n8
Svendsen, Lars 32–33

symbol 26, 29–31, 40, 47, 53, 61, 69, 78, 85, 113, 27n7, 30n16, 69n49

talking-about 1–3, 7, 43, 51, 64, 4n11
talking-to 1–3, 7–9, 43, 51, 64, 4n11
Talmud 18–19, 50
tools 6, 17–19, 22, 27, 42, 95–96, 103–105, 107, 109–110
toy 84–85, 88, 91–92
trees 2, 11, 58–59, 61–69, 71, 73–74, 76, 100, 104
Tronto, Joan 15n2

Uexküll, Jakob Johann von 38n45
Ury, Lesser 97–98, 102

Voltaire 74–75

Wolfson, Elliot 18, 116–117, 120, 49n45, 54n66
womb 36, 82–84
Wundt, Wilhelm 75, 99n17

Zionism 97, 81n18

DUSTIN N. ATLAS is Director of Jewish Studies and Associate Professor in the School of Religion at Queen's University. He specializes in contemporary Jewish thought and aesthetics, especially works that concern imperfection, gossip, and nonhuman creatures.

For Indiana University Press

Sabrina Black, Editorial Assistant
Tony Brewer, Artist and Book Designer
Anna Francis, Assistant Acquisitions Editor
Anna Garnai, Production Coordinator
Samantha Heffner, Marketing and Publicity Manager
Katie Huggins, Production Manager
Gigi Lamm, Director of Sales and Marketing
Alyssa Nicole Lucas, Marketing and Publicity Manager
Darja Malcolm-Clarke, Project Manager/Editor
Annie L. Martin, Editorial Director
Dan Pyle, Online Publishing Manager
Michael Regoli, Director of Publishing Operations
Jennifer L. Wilder, Senior Artist and Book Designer

www.ingramcontent.com/pod-product-compliance
Lightning Source LLC
Chambersburg PA
CBHW030625230426
43661CB00053B/2151